About the author

In 1980 Clare Maria Campbell completed a counselling course at City University, while working as a freelance journalist for a number of women's magazines. This interest in counselling and her commitment to working with women suffering emotional distress led her to being trained as a registered counsellor with the British Pregnancy Advisory Service in London where she worked for two years. In 1984 she became the agony aunt of *Company* magazine which provided the ideal solution of combining her dual interest in counselling and journalism. She also contributes to a range of other magazines and is working on a book about teenagers. She lives in Wandsworth in South London with her twin daughters.

SNAKES AND LADDERS

A Guide to Women's Emotional Health

Clare Maria Campbell

CENTURY

LONDON MELBOURNE AUCKLAND JOHANNESBURG

First published in 1988 by Century Hutchinson Ltd
Brookmount House, 62–65 Chandos Place,
London WC2N 4NW

Century Hutchinson Australia (Pty) Ltd
PO BOX 496, 16–22 Church Street, Hawthorn,
Victoria 3122, Australia

Century Hutchinson New Zealand Ltd
PO Box 40–086, 32–34 View Road, Glenfield,
Auckland 10, New Zealand

Century Hutchinson South Africa (Pty) Ltd
PO Box 337, Bergvlei, 2012 South Africa

Set by Avocet Marketing Services, Bicester, Oxon.
Printed and bound in Great Britain by
Anchor Brendon Ltd, Tiptree, Essex

British Library Cataloguing in Publication Data

Campbell, Clare Maria
    Snakes and ladders: a guide to women's
    emotional health.
    1. Women—Psychology 2. Emotions
    I. Title
    155.6'33   HQ1206

ISBN 0-7126-1845-7

Contents

Introduction

The emotional landscape of the late eighties is pockmarked and blasted. Some great battle has been fought here but no victory won. The sisterhood of agony aunts (of which I count myself a member) are the stretcher-bearers and ambulance drivers. We are not very noble, no ladies with lamps certainly, but at least we are there to provide first aid to patch up the emotional wounds which life can inflict on women or, if the wounds are too deep, pass them down the line to the dressing station for professional help.

As an agony aunt for a women's magazine I am close to this front line. I'm presented all the time with women's problems – nobody writes to say how happy she is. I try to provide the appropriate counsel and convince someone who is unhappy that she is not alone – there are plenty of people out there who can help and, perhaps just as important, millions of other women who are experiencing or have experienced exactly the same thing.

In our highly developed society, with doctors, psychoanalysts and the pharmaceutical industry offering so much professional help and support, why should this kind of safety net be necessary? Why can a letter to a magazine or newspaper journalist, to be published for complete strangers to see, articulate anguish which cannot be spoken between two ostensibly loving individuals? Why have so many self-help groups and specialist agencies sprung up and blossomed, the great majority of them run by women for women! Why indeed do women seem so especially vulnerable?

Very often a deeply unhappy woman will write to me with a

1

familiar story. Whatever the cause of the unhappiness it is often compounded by the fact that 'no one will listen', that a male partner (sometimes even her doctor) will put it all down to nerves, a period, the menopause – 'hormones'. How many times in how many marital rows have the words, 'don't be silly you're just being emotional' been sourly offered?

There is a plane of women's experience which we would all immediately recognize as being a key signifier of our gender. Not that women feel and men don't, not that men are no less compelled in their behaviour by testosterone and adrenalin than women are by their hormonal rhythms, but when it comes to *displaying* emotions, women are allowed much more license than men are.

The difference is one of perception – women are more 'emotional' than men because they are seen to be. People expect us to be, it's an overwhelmingly strong part of our culture. Women's magazines carry agony columns. Men's magazines don't. Mother's little helper is a pot of tranquillizers or a furtive swig from the sideboard. Daddy's down the pub. Big boys don't cry, or if they do, they don't talk about it, whereas women will often talk about their feelings to other women more freely than they will to men. Women test out new friendships with other women by seeing how far they can go in revealing old hurts or new happiness . . . of which men may be the cause, but men are excluded from this arena of emotional self-revelation. When husbands and lovers 'won't listen', other women will, even if it should be a magazine agony aunt who is doing the listening and, by inference, thousands of other completely anonymous women readers.

An agony aunt's mailbag reveals just how wide and deep is the range of problems encountered by ordinary women in their lives. A letter writer typically nearly always think that they are uniquely miserable, or their behaviour particularly obsessive, or their heartbreak utterly inconsolable. Am I normal? is a question asked over and over again. A key part of the counsel offered in reply therefore, and in the healing process itself, is in sharing the problem and breaking down the feeling of aloneness.

How to do this? Looking at the span of a woman's life from puberty onwards there are points in which, either by choice or with no choice offered, the pressures begin to pile on. That's life of course and it would be very boring and bland if there were no peaks and troughs, but there are troughs which are too deep. It is from here, often in tones of real despair, that an agony aunt hears the cries for help.

But looking at those pressure points is a very useful first step in communicating an answer to someone, to show her first that she's in the same boat as a lot of other people and that how she has coped with life to date is just as important. It's a good way of demonstrating that the crisis that has triggered the cry for help is going to pass, that a troubled or unhappy woman's underlying emotional health can be as robust as anyone else's.

Emotional health is not just about problems or the crisis that strikes when you are least able to cope, just as healthy eating is not about crash diets. Emotional health is for all our lives, it is about happiness as much as unhappiness and is something to preserve and cherish so as to be able to cope at all with inevitable crises and pressures.

Women who have coped well with the early stages of stress tend to cope just as well when it comes back, to be good survivors as much as achievers. Others who have fallen at the first fence also tend to fail again or be especially vulnerable to stress and pressure in new forms.

If there is 'unfinished business' with parents, family, authority, lovers or friends it can come back to endanger new relationships with husbands and children many years later. For example many teenage anorexics, compulsive non-eaters, may seem to recover in young adulthood but relapse again after childbirth in their early thirties, or they may transfer their obsessive behaviour to alcoholism.

This handbook of emotional health is firmly based on an agony aunt's experience of the real problems of real people. Only their names have been changed to respect personal privacy. I would like to take this opportunity of paying tribute to all who were concerned enough with the way women live their lives and the way they will be living them tomorrow for agreeing to share their experiences here in the hope that others may benefit. The book is designed to be a practical guide to scaling the ladders and avoiding slipping down the snakes. It proves that, whatever the problem, you're not alone, there are plenty who feel the way you do and, if the going gets really tough and emotional first aid isn't enough, it tells you where to go for advice and support – friends and family foremost, then the many organizations offering specialist advice and support.

1

The end of childhood

Girls on the brink of becoming women are a group that primitive societies regard with a special awe. Awakening sexuality is equated with magic. A girl's first menstrual blood marks the beginning of the end of her childhood. It is also the symbolic evidence of her developing sexuality, and as such, has been treated as a rite of initiation by many cultures throughout the history of womankind. The taboos and the terror of 'bad blood' that still exist in many societies even today, have been the subject of much theorising on man's fears about the mysteries of female fertility.

Fortunately, for Western women of the late twentieth century, these fears have been pushed to the margin of our culture, but the onset of menstruation is still a time when a girl needs sensitive treatment by those around her, particularly by her parents and by her peers at school. One of the difficulties in explaining menstruation to pre-pubescent girls is that every woman's experience of it is different. Considering the universality of the experience, the number of individual variations of that experience seems as great as the variations in the human face. The biological explanation is simple but the individual experience of it is far more complex as the physiological and emotional effects blur into one. It's not surprising that tempers fray and nerves tauten if heads ache and backs hurt, if breasts and bellies seem bloated and spots, nausea and fatigue interrupt the pattern of a young life. Mood changes can range from slight irritability to what some doctors claim can amount to murderous rage.

Worrying about these internal upheavals just adds to the

problem, which is why it is so important that periods are shown to be a natural part of everyday life. 'Old wives' tales' (more likely to be told in the playground than by old wives) just serve to reinforce bad feelings. I have received many letters from grown up women who trace back fears of sex, of pregnancy and giving birth to a lack of hard information about menstruation at the time when they needed it most – puberty. If school sex education is not up to scratch and parents are reluctant and shy, a sympathetic and sensitive family doctor (preferably female) is probably the best person to explain the physiological and emotional effects that menstruation can have on a girl's body.

Our society treats adolescent girls as consumers – their awakening sexuality is equated with pop stars and make-up, with reasons to spend money. The internal messages being sent by the bodies of pubescent girls are met by a mass of external messages being sent by the adult world, by their parents, by their teachers, by their girlfriends, by their boyfriends, by magazines and by television – messages about how they should behave, look and feel, and what they should be.

The pressures of this kind of bombardment are intense, and all this happens as adolescent girls are moving through their teens to the point where rebellion against parental values is the first and necessary step to reaching adult 'freedom', attaining responsibility at the expense of parental protection.

We have to reject the value systems of our parents while desperately searching for a viable one of our own – the more different, the more wild and outlandish, the better. In the midst of this confusion we are also trying to find a role for ourselves that fits not just with our family's demands and expectations but with our friends and our sexuality.

The transition can be especially difficult for a girl who has been brought up to believe that by deferring her needs to others she will be cared for in return. Subconsciously she avoids personal responsibility until suddenly her security is stripped away and she is left standing alone and vulnerable on the edge of a hostile world. It is not surprising that many girls experience something approaching real terror at the prospect of stepping over the line into adulthood, feelings that can sometimes cause a woman to cling to childhood and push back 'growing up' until her body takes the decision for her.

Luise Eichenbaum and Susie Orbach identify these conflicting expectations in their book *Understanding Women*:

Girls rarely experience encouragement and support for gestures of autonomy. More often than not, girls move out into the world accompanied by prohibitions, cautions, restrictions, fears, rather than expectations of success and acceptance.

Just when we most need an inner resource of self-confidence to be able to take fundamental decisions about our future, we feel fear and doubt about our personal worth as women and our ability to function independently. On the practical side there are important choices to be made about school, college, university and employment (or the lack of it). Adolescence is also the time when we reassess our relations with parents and with friends of both sexes. These changes and fluctuations in our feelings about others place a tremendous strain on our own growing, but precarious, sense of who we really are.

SEXUAL IDENTITY
Central to this struggle is the question of sexual identity. Heterosexuality is no longer the only permissible choice that polite society allows but, in the post-AIDS environment and with the rising incidence of other sexually transmitted diseases, we need to be doubly sure that we are making our own decisions about how, when, where and who we want sex with, including the question of whether we want it at all.

Such decisions should not be instantaneous. Sexuality is not static. As we change, grow and develop emotionally we may find our preference for either sex altering too. Finding a sexual role we feel happy with can take time, and experience of close friendships with both male and female. Nor do these have to be physical. Adolescence is a time of searching, both for what we want from ourselves, from others and the outside world. It is also the time when we begin to realize that we may have to give back in return. The hallmark of a first mature relationship with either sex is our ability to put someone else's needs before our own.

Despite much theorising, no one really knows what makes men and women be homosexual or bisexual. 'Coming out' or revealing a homosexual identity can be a very stressful process, particularly for a young person who will have little enough self-confidence anyway. Having a sympathetic listener around, someone who's going to be as objective as possible (and that more often than not excludes parents) is important and there are numerous specialist support agencies (listed in the reference section) who offer sympathetic and informed advice to adolescents who feel lost in their search for their own sexual identity. Workshops where it is possible to explore these hidden feelings in depth can also help to dispel some of the emotional confusion.

SEXUAL INITIATION

Whatever doubts some of us may feel about their sexual preference, the big question confronting most young women is if or when they are going to begin an active sex life. The law rules that no male should have sex with a girl he knows to be under sixteen. Apart from the law, consent to sexual intercourse is the most intimate right of the individual. But like all intensely personal issues, this also makes clearcut decisions or moral choices very difficult. Force of personality can result in 'rape' as much as physical aggression, but there is no redress under the law for being charmed or bullied into bed.

A burden of guilt carried sometime in the future for consent too freely given is going to mar the process of growing into a mature and self-respecting adult. And it is possible to avoid such burdens if we just give ourselves time to make up our minds about why we want to have sex with a particular person and whether it is a considered decision or one made under peergroup pressure.

My letters give evidence of the large numbers of young people who still seem to think that sex is compulsory by a certain age. Good sex requires self-esteem, relaxation, and patience, qualities which do not come easily to the average teenager. Sex without passion is not only not as good as sex with, it is also a waste of a unique moment of initiation. There's enough emotional turmoil going on in adolescence without the regret and the self-depreciation of sex for sex's sake.

The internal pressures of a teenage girl's world, allied with the unstoppable progression towards the responsibility of being a young adult, can prove too much. When such a case shows up as a cry for help, her letter to me often expresses a sense of shame that she should feel this kind of anxiety at all, and she finds it terribly hard to admit to anyone, even those closest to her. She suppresses her feelings because she thinks they show weakness and confirm her already low estimate of her personal worth.

Seventeen-year-old Jenny came from an outwardly stable and reasonably happy middle-class, well-off background. Her mother and father, both solicitors, were proud of their daughter's academic achievements and were looking forward to her following in their footsteps to read law at an Oxbridge college.

Jenny was attractive, intelligent, open, cheerful and socially successful, but within the space of a year she became quiet, restive and withdrawn. Her parents began to start worrying, was this just adolescent angst or was it something deeper? Jenny thought she knew what was wrong:

I have a problem that may sound trivial but is ruining my life. I have always had an inferiority complex, but now I feel it more acutely, because at my age it is important to get along socially with people . . . I feel so inadequate that I just can't accept myself for what I am and imagine that people automatically dislike me even though I know it isn't true. Is there anything I can do, or any organization that can help me?

You don't have to be seventeen to have such feelings of inadequacy but how we cope with them first time round will have an affect on how we cope with them in later life. Adolescence is when such feelings start to crowd in and when, because all we've got to compare them with are the departed certainties of childhood, they can seem most desperate. A word or two of reassurance, an affirmation that we are not alone in our anxiety are sometimes all it takes, but if these phantoms are not exorcized, they can return in new and more frightening guises such as eating disorders like anorexia, panic attacks and depression.

There is a level of support to be found in such circumstances from friends, family or even an outside counselling service, but there are simple measures of self-help that Jenny could put into effect. Her sense of inadequacy is irrational. She knows this herself and yet feels powerless to do anything about it. There are some simple ways in which we can tap that elusive inner self that provides its own safety net of common sense.

Other people can reassure us because they reinforce perceptions about ourselves that we know to be true but which our emotional confusion has caused us to doubt. External reassurance is great if you can get it (and, of course, believe in it) but what if it's not there, or the other people in question such as a mother, father or boyfriend are the direct source of the feelings of inadequacy? Jenny felt people disliked her but the evidence of her large group of friends pointed to the contrary. Outside reassurance didn't help. The solution would have to come from within herself.

She began by quite simply trying to separate what she felt from what she knew. She even wrote it down, like a shopping list, the qualities she rationally 'knew' she had, even though her feelings were shrieking the opposite. She listed her achievements, however insignificant ... they began to add up. Jenny wrote subsequently:

When I first looked at what I had written, it seemed alien to me, as though I was describing someone else. But gradually it seemed to sink in and I began to identify with this apparently popular and competent person. It was me I was describing and, for the first time, I began to like and respect myself.

Jenny had managed to avoid the first snake of her adolescence and climb the first rung of the ladder alone. That achievement in itself will contribute towards her self-confidence in later life and her ability to cope with subsequent crises.

Adolescence is the first time that we are forced to confront ourselves as individuals, separate from, and no longer protected by, our family and friends. The world is out there waiting for us and, as we have seen, we may not always have the courage to face it head on. Our parents' attitude towards our new autonomy is also ambivalent; they want us to be successful and happy but at the same time are frightened about whether we will use our freedom responsibly, and about their own approaching redundancy as we lose our dependence upon them.

These kinds of tensions can build up in a family and even by our early to mid-teens we are already carrying 'unfinished business' with us from the past. From the moment we first open our eyes on the world we start learning to relate to the people around us. This process has a knock-on effect so that each relationship formed affects the next one. Our emotional security hinges on these first contacts with the outside world and determines our attitude towards it as adults. Unfair as it may seem, how we approach new people as well as new experiences is forever dependent upon that vital primary relationship – usually with our mothers. The significance of this for women is such that I have devoted a later section solely to mother – daughter relationships and their effect on later life, but all parental concern, however well meaning, is going to have some form of impact.

Young women writing to me are often confused by parental criticism, which they interpret as lack of affection. Rachel was eighteen when she first became aware of the widening rift between her and her parents. Her elder brother had always been regarded by the family as the 'difficult' and rebellious one whereas Rachel had thrived on the approval of authority both at home and at school. However, adolescence brought a sudden and overwhelming envy of the attention her brother's behaviour always seemed to attract. She went punk, eagerly embracing all the symbols and signifiers of youth rebellion made tribal – pink hair, safety-pins, gobbing, swearing, the lot. Of course, her parents were horrified, as Rachel intended them to be, but it didn't make her any happier:

I have always had a good relationship with my parents, but just lately it

11

has deteriorated rapidly. They seem to have become distrustful of me and continually comment on my taste in clothes. I considered leaving home, but they were so upset by this that I dropped the idea for the time being. I am so confused I don't know whether they want me to live my own life or go back to being their 'good little girl'.

This of course was as tough for the parents as it was for the suffering adolescent because they indeed wanted both. They wished for a daughter who was both fulfilled and responsible, yet who still had needs that only they could satisfy. Paradoxically Rachel's 'bad' brother became the link that united them once more as a family.

Eventually he was able to interpret those feelings Rachel found impossible to express to her parents herself. In the end Rachel was able to retain her independence but she also felt for the first time that she was loved in her own right rather than because of her deference towards others.

For many others the passage through adolescence is a journey without a happy end. The unhappy teenager who cannot work through her problematic relationships is the one prone to later emotional disturbance, as illustrated in the case of thirty-four-year-old Joanne:

Please advise me on handling criticism. I have feared and hated it since I was thirteen. My parents told me I was too fat at fourteen and I became anorexic. Later I fell in love with a man I loved very much but whose critical comments caused me to attempt suicide.

Now I have an interesting job and am engaged to a gentle, kind and sympathetic man. He hasn't criticized me yet but surely this is too good to last.

Identifying and understanding that first crisis could have prevented years of feelings of inadequacy, instigated perfectly innocently by her family. I am not suggesting that we go in for lifelong psychoanalysis or update those around us on the state of our feelings with bulletins on the hour every hour, but it has to be true that an awareness of our own vulnerability in adolescence, and the vulnerability of others when we ourselves are parents, may avert the ripple effect that we see in Joanne's story of old hurts going on hurting.

It is as stupid as it is unkind to expect the young to cope alone with all the anxieties and inadequacies, real or imagined, that beset them at a time when both their bodies and their emotions are captains of their existence.

Those with a strongly developed sense of self seem to survive better, some waiver then regain their footing, but there are some whose trouble is too deep, whose emotional problem too inconsolable to be worked through. It won't just be a matter of sulks, hurts and passing adolescent tantrums, but compulsive behaviour patterns protracted to a degree which can be genuinely life endangering. One of the darkest of these threats is anorexia.

Anorexia

Much has been written about the so-called 'slimming disease', why it affects teenage girls in particular and why especially those from comparatively well-off social backgrounds. Much has still to be understood. Is the compulsion to slim to do with the urge to conform to what some outside commercial role-model which tells a girl how she should look and how she should be, or is it a deeper compulsion to deny the onset of sexuality? Approximately one in two hundred adolescent girls is at risk from anorexia. Its close companion, bulimia (compulsive binge eating) also stalks the teenage bedrooms of suburbia. A classic pattern for supposedly 'recovered' teenage anorexics as they get older is to swing from one illness to the other and back again, starving and stuffing by turns.

One step on the way to understanding must be the significance of a woman's perception of her own body to her increasing emotional maturity. As our hormones begin to dictate terms in adolescence, we have to accept loss of control, not just in the internal sense of the menstrual cycle, but in the sense that our bodies are no longer just our own. They are public property, alien objects to be admired, assessed, compared, praised, criticized or damned by our own friends, by our boyfriends, by parents and, of course subjectively, by the sternest critic of all, ourselves.

Even after two decades of feminism, a woman's body is a powerful signifier of 'success' or 'failure'. Look at the fashion of the past twenty years; designers have idealised the primal unformed bodyscreen of prepubescence, making big, grown-up girls pursue the impossible – to be undernourished but healthy and aged thirteen for life.

The whole slimming thing, in spite of the injection of a good deal of nutritional common sense in the past few years, remains a close adjunct of the fashion and cosmetic industries, even if 'health' is also now big business. With the female form so commercialized and every teen-media outlet shouting 'this is how you should be', it is therefore hardly surprising that a girl's body should sometimes be a battleground in a struggle for self-identity. To a teenager with no other means of expression, her body is all she has and, like a political prisoner, the ultimate weapon in her struggle for power is to go on hunger strike.

Alison is twenty and feels fully recovered from the disease. She also feels that she has learnt important lessons about herself from her experience. She effected her own recovery, without resorting either to counselling or to 'family therapy', after the sudden realization that she was 'tired of nonparticipation in my own life'. The onset of anorexia had begun at fourteen when she had started to accumulate the so-called puppyfat of puberty. Always sensitive to criticism, the jokey but barbed remarks of her friends and family made her determined to starve herself to 'make them sorry for the things they'd said'.

Gradually Alison discovered that the illness she had nurtured as a comfort and ally had turned into a life-threatening enemy. As the pressures of exams and relations with boyfriends began to increase, she relied increasingly on controlling her weight. Her periods stopped. She became more and more silent. Her family alternatively tried bullying and beseeching her to eat but Alison would not budge.

She says now that somewhere in her mass of confused feelings, 'If I could only hang on to this one area of control in my life, everything else would follow and I would be happy'. Fortunately there was sudden diversion on her path to self-destruction when someone else started to matter more to her than her obsession with food:

14

From the minute we met, I felt safer and more self-confident. The strangest thing was that my weight no longer seemed important and I just started to eat normally again. I had felt odd before, as though my life had gone out of focus. It was as though a positive force was suddenly switched on inside me again which directed my thoughts outside myself. My thoughts became clear. I knew I wanted to feel warm, loved and alive.

Alison's boyfriend was not the cure so much as the catalyst which let her take command of her life again. She was very lucky. For many families the hardest task is persuading the anorexic that she has a problem at all. Once she actively seeks help of her own volition the sufferer is already well on the way back to health.

Why is it that so many young women (only 10 per cent of young males in proportion to girls become anorexic) have to pay such a dreadful price? Adolescent girls are especially vulnerable to the media pressures to conform to some impossible ideal (as well as rebel against family strictures). There is a whole marketing industry of teen magazines and teen products based on this fact. Getting better is about leaving this stage behind, gaining emotional maturity and assuming responsibility. The anorexic must be allowed to let her illness go and replace it with a range of positive goals which matter far more than proving you can control your body weight. The environment must be sufficiently 'safe' to do this without depriving the anorexics of what little responsibility for herself she has remaining. Mature women who can admit to their desires can deal with eating disorders on their own terms, but we cannot expect adolescents to do it alone.

It is no coincidence that low self-esteem is a common factor in anorexia, and in the compulsive, destructive behaviour patterns that can develop later, such as drug dependency and alcoholism. The emotional earthquakes of adolescence can produce seismic echoes in later life, but if we can be sure or be reassured by others of our self-image and self-identity when young, then the antibodies against later assaults are already in the system. Until we know, like and respect ourselves, it is terribly difficult to form a satisfactory relationship with anyone else. If a relationship damages that self-respect then it can be a sad and mutually destructive affair. This is one of the many painful lessons of teenage love.

Young love, self-knowledge and the journey into adulthood

At the age of only nineteen Caroline was already suffering from bouts of depression brought on by a succession of failed relationships, all of which seemed to stem from an unhappy first love affair. She was deeply hurt when her boyfriend rejected her, but found it difficult to talk about how she felt even to her closest friends and family. The result of her unresolved conflict was confusion and an inability to form another satisfying or happy relationship. Purely because she had slept with her first and much-adored boyfriend, Caroline felt compelled to sleep with four subsequent men without having the slightest desire to do so, sexually or emotionally. She felt guilty, ashamed, she began to actually hate herself.

When she finally met someone else that she both liked and felt very sexually attracted to, she became even more confused because she had come to disassociate love and sex. She also felt powerless to do anything that might break her destructive behaviour pattern:

I know that I will probably give in to this man and then regret it. I used to look forward to seeing him, but now I feel that it's all been spoilt.

Other people's opinions of us don't matter half so much as the way we feel about ourselves, but adolescent and young adult women are especially vulnerable to attack on both fronts, from inside as well as from outside. Caroline had lost sight of her real self after her first unhappy affair, then she sank into increasing depression and self-depreciation. She was ashamed of having had sex with several men, not because she felt herself to be promiscuous but because she wanted love as well. Experience taught her that the two could be isolated from one another and her disillusionment soon turned into a distrust of all men, allied with a hatred of herself.

Before she began to feel better Caroline had to recognize these feelings and accept that love was going to be an essential element of any affair for her. Her conflict originated from acting out of character but the first thing she needed to establish was what her real character was and to like it.

Gradually, through talking to a counsellor, Caroline was able to rediscover her self-respect and allow a new relationship to develop naturally, without having to respond to ultimatums for sex and her accompanying self-loathing for giving in.

The traumas of first love and first sex can do more than some gentle ego-bruising, they can do lasting damage, but there are ways young people, and those who care for them, can turn the turmoil of adolescent love into life-enhancing and personality -reinforcing experiences.

Twenty-year-old Margaret had had what she considered to be a stable, equal and loving relationship with Mike since she was sixteen. They had often talked about the future, Mike always making the assumption that Margaret would follow wherever he led. They were both language students and as they came to take their final exams, Margaret had become increasingly interested in pursuing a career as a travel courier. This would involve long periods of time away from Mike, and when she tentatively mentioned the idea, he dismissed it out of hand. Margaret felt sullen and resentful but was incapable of expressing her anger. He threatened her with breaking off the relationship entirely if she did not give up her plan. They argued but there was no resolution – meanwhile Margaret began to suffer from clinical anxiety symptoms:

Mike's disapproval seemed to negate my existence. I began to suffer from sudden attacks of panic at the thought of being without him. He seemed the puppet-master without whom I would be personally powerless. I think he thought I would come crawling back, but during our time apart I slowly began to realize that all the opinions and perceptions I believed to be my own had been based on his. He was no more to blame for this than I was. It seems sad that I could only discover my self-confidence and personal strength by finishing our affair. He couldn't accept my independence and accused me of having found someone else. I saw then that I had no intrinsic value to Mike. I was merely something that another man had stolen from him.

17

Margaret got out of it her way. The end of a four-year affair was sad, certainly. It left wounds but not scars because Margaret had grown up enough to realize the inequality of the partnership and the danger of her being stifled by it before she had even started adult life in any real sense. She saw her self-identity threatened but had enough of it left intact to fight off the depression and the panic attacks (engendered ironically by the fear of losing him) and, in the end, make her own stand. She was also lucky in having emotional support from other friends and from her family. They provided reassurance – in the first place, that she was right to assert her own ambition and, in the second, that she had a personality other than that for which Mike pulled the strings. They provided somewhere safe to shelter as the emotional storms of having to disengage from him broke over her.

The mutual exploring of sex underpins much of young love. Since physical attraction is often the primary basis of an early affair it is inevitable that these feelings, wondrous and frightening at the same time, may evaporate as quickly as they blossomed. The onset of maturity, the first glimmers of adult wisdom, come from the ability to separate the image of love from the substance, to think not of tonight or next week but of lasting attachment and ultimately, of course, the responsibility of being a parent oneself.

YOUNG SEX AND YOUNG PREGNANCY

Talking about adolescent and young adult women in a developed Western society, I am blandly assuming that all pregnancies below the age of, say, twenty-one are unexpected (not necessarily unwanted), in or out of marriage, although that remains quite an assumption to make. In any event, the impact of an unexpected pregnancy at *any* time in a woman's life should not be under-estimated. Teenagers have even less ability to deal with the emotional turmoil of an unplanned pregnancy, and minimal awareness of the impact decisions made in the eye of this storm will have on the rest of their lives.

The state of sex education still leaves much to be desired and many of the young women writing to me feel they don't know enough about effective contraception, nor do they have the option of saying 'no' (although the spectres of AIDS and cervical cancer now seem to offer them grim support). Having a basic knowledge of contraception (see pp. 137-40) is of course vital to avoiding the potential traumas of teenage pregnancy and abortion but there's more to it than that.

It's a question of allowing young people responsibility for, and an understanding of, the emotional consequences of their physical actions. The preceding case histories have shown some of the traumas that follow when sex and love become split in two, but some young people have their own minds made up very firmly indeed, they just want sex, and the consequences can be tossed aside. Such individuals may or may not be tougher than the rest, but the majority of young adult women are going to operate on the emotional plane as well as the sexual one . . . and they are capable of being emotionally damaged if things go wrong. No more so perhaps than by the experience of abortion.

ABORTION

From my experience as a pregnancy counsellor I came to realize that an unplanned pregnancy was a possibility for any sexually active woman of childbearing age, whatever form of contraceptive she may or may not have been using. Women who were aware of that possibility coped more easily with the crisis of an unwanted pregnancy than those who thought their method of contraception had made them 100 per cent safe.

An unexpected pregnancy is a time of acute crisis for any woman. For a young adult, nothing so effectively slams the door on childhood. Nothing can reach so reassuringly deeply to the heart of one's womanliness as a pregnancy, yet at the same time send such confusing messages about one's own identity and future purpose. A woman can feel terrifyingly alone when she's got the beginnings of somebody else inside her.

As I walked, I thought about having a baby, and in that state of total inebriation it seemed to me that a baby might be no such bad thing, however impractical and impossible. My sister had babies. There was no reason why I shouldn't have one either, it would serve me right, I thought for being born a woman in the first place. I couldn't pretend that I wasn't a woman, could I, however much I might try from day to day to avoid the issue?

If you thought that read slightly better than the average problem-page letter you would be right. It's from a work of fiction, Margaret Drabble's *The Millstone*. It communicates very well just how much having a child is still seen as the justification for a woman's existence.

Pregnancy is the great reminder of our traditional role as mothers and nurturers. It is too ancient and powerful a mythology to be easily cast aside. Feminism won a woman's right to choose but dragged a fearsome responsibility in its wake.

As a political issue abortion is overexposed yet discussion of abortion as personal experience is avoided. After the event, perhaps many years after, women may be able to confide in their husband (more often in fact their female friends) about the terrors and traumas of an abortion in their teens or early twenties, 'the emotion, guilt, pain and silence women have when they choose termination' as Angela Neustatter says in her book *Mixed Feelings*, but even the most emotionally mature woman may prefer to shunt such an experience into some secret recess of the mind.

Neustatter's book charts and analyses some of these ambivalent attitudes of women (including herself) towards their own experience of abortion and its after effect on their lives. Writing of her own experience she says:

For several months afterwards I experienced a curious upheaval of the emotions, an unaccustomed sense of nihilism; a turbulence in my private life which I felt unable to control. The feelings subsided and passed. I still regret not having been able to have the third child. I still think about it, but I am sure it was not the wrong decision just a sad one.

No one can accompany us through the trauma of terminating a pregnancy but a majority of women find talking to a trained counsellor goes some way in lessening the distress. The very fact that the counsellor is a stranger can be a positive factor in lessening the burden of guilt and fear.

Nineteen-year-old Frances had always found it easy to express her feelings and anxieties to both her family and friends but pregnancy drastically altered her attitude. She had been brought up as a strict Catholic and her moral conflict over what she knew would be considered as murder by those close to her was intensified by a sensation of terrifying isolation:

I felt that I had no right to support from anyone since what I was contemplating was such a dreadful sin. I suppose I thought I ought to be made to suffer.

When Frances talked to a counsellor she was able to separate her feelings of religious guilt from the responsibility for her personal destiny, the freedom to choose, that society had granted her:

Once I could see the situation in perspective I knew I must accept both the responsibility for what I was doing and the inevitable guilt – but it suddenly seemed more bearable.

Knowing what the operation itself entails is also important in dispelling fear and guilt. The counsellor should provide calm, clear and concise factual information on the practical details of an abortion (see pp. 123-5), something which goes a long way to reassuring a woman already under stress.

In spite of all the hurt, abortion is one area of our lives where the right to make our own decisions about if and when to bear children has been won. Even if the emotional cost can be high, this responsibility can, in fact, strengthen self-confidence and result in a positive outcome.

Frances wrote later:

I knew I would never be the same again. I have suffered a wound so deep that the scar is not going to disappear. But I also know that I can learn to live with it and, in a strange way, I have more self-respect through having survived it.

SEXUALLY TRANSMITTED DISEASES

Young women write to me for reassurance. There are times when saying 'Don't worry, it's not going to happen to you'

21

doesn't work or is inappropriate. Never was there a more apt case in point than when they write about their terror of contracting AIDS, a fear which hangs over us all like a grey cloud, infecting not so much our bodies but our minds with the contagion of suspicion. The initial complacency that the disease was something to do with homosexuals and drug-abusers has given way to real fear, driven by media frenzy of the 'gay plague' variety and the government's exhortation that we should not 'die of ignorance'.

There's enough good, clear information around on safe sex to make repetition here unnecessary but what of the emotional consequences of AIDS? 'On me, not in me' is the message, 'clever girls carry a condom' say the magazines, but the urge to merge in the act of intercourse is primevally strong. Other forms of lovemaking can be very enjoyable but not, perhaps, when we feel that our partners are petrified of full penetration, or of coming into the slightest contact with any bodily fluid, whether it be blood, semen or saliva. (See pages 128-130.)

We face the prospect of a future society that only the strictest of religious rulings has ever sought to create, the possibility of a world in which intercourse is reserved solely for reproduction within the confines of a completely faithful partnership.

What if you don't have a partner? How do young people in particular navigate the shoals of sex, love and marriage to find an 'ideal' partner with the fear of AIDS stalking them?

Cultures long derided, in which marriages are arranged, suddenly look less primitive. In the promiscuous, 'liberated' West the outcome could be less cosy, not because sex before marriage is essential to its subsequent success, but because of the distrust and suspicion that AIDS instils in our minds about human beings around us – that casual conversation, did he just show a lively interest in my past or was he conducting a forensic examination of my sexual history? That flu he complained of – could it be? . . . No, don't be silly.

Already the psychological effects of the great fear are showing up in my postbag. Ignorance of the basic facts is partly to blame, fear of sharing cups and glasses, toothbrushes and so on, is common but what is more deeply disturbing is the growing fear of being touched at all.

AIDS is not a media invention. We have to come to terms with it for the foreseeable future, but it should not be allowed to taint our minds with fear to the extent that the capacity for loving, human relationships is destroyed. So what can we do to safe-guard ourselves without promoting panic – while at the same time getting on with the realities of life, love and sex? A positive and informed approach is a more sensible attitude to the 'belt and braces' approach of chastity and condoms, and the ability to be frank (and the ability to trust) what partners tell each other about their sexual proclivities and number of partners is obviously going to be very important.

Rampant promiscuity is obviously out except for those with a deathwish. That includes men, whether homosexual, bisexual or heterosexual. Men must reassess their sexual mores too, one result of the disease being that women will be far more sus-picious of men as to their 'fitness for sexual consumption'. The breakthrough in understanding comes from the realization that all promiscuity is dangerous. Today's young woman may spend little time on moral agonizing over whether to go to bed with a man or not, but the fear of AIDS (and herpes and cervical cancer) provides a powerful contraceptive. What the patterns of meeting, loving and living with sexual partners will be in a decade's time is hard to predict, the only certainty is that the patterns of human sexual relationships are going to change as radically as they did in the sixties with the advent of the Pill.

The emerging woman

We cannot gain relief from emotional pain until we acknowledge its existence. Acceptance of this fact is an integral part of the rites of passage into the next stage of growth. It requires the slow shedding, one by one, of our childhood illusions of a secure and stable adult world. It is also a matter of choice. We can easily ignore the message of our experience by pretending that nothing has changed. Some of us managed perfectly adequately all our lives as self-deluding permanent adolescents but in the end it is a suffocating existence. The getting of wisdom is always worth the struggle.

The growth of personality does not have a beginning, a middle and an end but is a far more gradual process of getting wisdom by appraising and recognizing the importance of what has been before, as well as looking forward to the future. Adolescence does not suddenly cease. Its central issues fade gradually into the background to be overlaid with the new preoccupations of adult life.

No one becomes an adult overnight however. For every one step forward there are two steps back. There is a powerful urge to break away and become independent but, just as we begin to find our feet, the world bares its teeth and sends us scurrying back into childhood.

Yet we quickly grow resentful of our own powerlessness and renew our attempts to escape. Those of us for whom an external crisis coincides with the internal crisis of adolescence, may find themselves 'compulsorily detained in childhood' and have to try far harder to find a road to freedom.

A crisis or 'life accident' as Gail Sheehy describes them in her book *Passages*, need not necessarily be harmful to a woman's long-term emotional health, but if it strikes during a period of natural vulnerability the chances of its leaving emotional scars is that much greater. Recognizing the weaknesses and the strengths of young women is the first step in minimizing the damage of such early life accidents as teenage pregnancy, abortion, anorexia and sexually transmitted disease.

There is one aspect of young love I have not tackled in great depth and that is marriage in the teens. In no way do I want to imply that young love and young marriage should be considered a 'snake' that might endanger long-term happiness and emotional fulfilment, but I would say this: as we have seen, out of adolescent turmoil often comes an urge to retreat back into childhood or somehow deflect the full blast of grown-up realities. A teenage marriage can seem to offer this apparent safety but rather than compel development it can postpone it by lengthening the financial, emotional and (especially if there's a baby around) physical dependence on our parents and can eventually prompt us to see our partner as some kind of captor.

The woman who breaks away soon learns how to survive

alone – she has to. A girl in adult disguise can only get away with it for so long – before she either resolves her inner conflict or faces the consequences of denying it.

2

Good times, bad times:
the twenties

The storms of adolescence are not all over on our twentieth
birthday. Some of us achieve a greater degree of maturity than
others by the end of our teens, while some haven't even started.
There are some who prefer never to enter the struggle at all but
at the potential cost of immolating their own personality and
losing their separate identity. It is 'easier' for young women than
young men to opt out at this stage because there is usually
someone around who will take care of them and in whose
interests it is, subconsciously or otherwise, to prevent or at least
delay their attainment of full adult autonomy.

An ambitious social survey conducted by the BBC for their
Lovelaw series in 1986 looked at patterns of love and marriage all
over the world and the differing expectations of couples entering
into it. It became overwhelmingly apparent that women expected
and got less out of marriage than men. They suffered under the
pressure of having to fulfil too many roles and from lack of
personal fulfilment if they had married young.

Men were happier with their lot on the whole because,
although they too might be role-prisoners as husband-father-
provider, they still made most of the internal family decisions,
had external control of the political and business world and were
much more able to assert their individuality without breaking the
cultural bounds of what was expected in family life.

The consumer-capitalist culture of ambition, struggle and the
worship of success of course reinforces these male expectations.
Women as yet do not have so many strong role-models as men;

they're either presented as sexual consumer durables, executive clones of men, in pinstripe and cameo brooches, or 'nurturers', blissfully ladling out baked beans in an eternally sunlit dream-kitchen. Men know they are expected to compete, most women still doubt they will even qualify for the race.

By the time men enter their twenties, therefore, they are likely to be equipped with a strong sense of personal direction and a certain amount of self-confidence. For women the possible paths to follow suddenly diverge at right angles to each other. Our twenties are a time of testing ourselves out on a world which is suddenly a much bigger and more challenging place than it was for us in our teens. It is also the time for crucial decisions – although these are often far less irrevocable than they might seem at the time.

So what are the choices confronting women at this stage and what are the underlying emotional influences which may affect our decisions? The world is supposedly opening up for women and, indeed, the range of choices, given a degree of economic independence (and that effectively means employment), is wide. Career, further education, love, living together, marriage, children now, children later, both or not at all? We have served our time of adolescent turmoil. We may have been emotionally bruised but we have recovered. We are sexually experienced. We have some money in our pocket. People are beginning to take us seriously. Now for the first time it seems we can determine our own lives, although absolute self-determination can sometimes be illusory.

There is a strong tug going on inside us, both to copy the life-patterns of our parents (assuming they had a conventional and stable relationship) and to continue that necessary teenage rebellion against their values and expectations of us – which may either be to establish a brilliant career or be an instant source of grandchildren or even, agonizingly – and this is not at all infrequent – both!

As in so many other phases of life these kinds of pressures are greater for women than for men. If we aim to succeed in a career we know we have to be that much better and that much more ambitiously tough than a man – and that we may either be forfeiting full-time motherhood or our hopes of having a family at all. If we choose early marriage and childbearing, no one can guarantee that we can ever get a clawhold back in the job market.

In spite of all these choices pressing in, life still seems pretty simple. Consider your options, choose the right answer, punch the right button and all should come right – that's how it can seem to a young adult who, at the same time, can be unsympathetic to those who don't happen to share these simplistically muscular ideals or those who, like many thirty and forty-year-old women with families, may be going through a genuine crisis. Such a crisis can be cruelly put down by a young adult as 'throwing a wobbler', a simple failure by an older woman to 'plan her life properly' – as if such a thing were possible.

The young woman in her early twenties will probably think that it is. Turbulent as these years can be they are usually less stressful than those which come before and after. What makes the difference is lack of doubt. In our twenties our capacity for reflection is not yet fully developed so we tend to get on towards our immediate goals rather than wobbling around on the sidelines wondering why we should want to play at all, let alone win.

'The prisoner's dilemma' – young motherhood

It is a brutal truth that what we consider to be 'love' at this stage is sometimes just an urge to submerge ourselves into another human being and avoid the realities of having to take decisions alone. Men fall prey to this temptation just as readily but it operates as less of a threat to their long-term development. If a man marries in his twenties he gains a supportive ally for his ambitions, a constant friend and lover on tap whenever he wants her. There is no way that a wife could detract from his development and progress in the world of work, which is the arena in which he can resolve any remaining conflicts about his identify or dependency on others in a far more positive way than he would in his marriage, home and family.

The woman who makes an early marriage is straightaway establishing a conflict for herself. She may have consciously rejected motherhood and already be mapping out a successful career but the imprint of the mother role-model is branded deep, far deeper than the 'independent' role-models established for women since the sixties. The question of having children is implicit in a marriage, but the dilemma is entirely the woman's – choose self-determination (and guilt for babies unborn), or self-immolation (and guilt for personal potential unfulfilled). Guilt and a certain amount of regret appears inescapable whichever path we choose and, if that guilt is blocked out, emotional problems can build up behind the dam.

Cathy was a newly-married graduate of twenty-three when she found out she was pregnant. She hadn't planned it this way. She could not imagine it happening to her – after all she was a scientist, a research chemist with big ambitions. She knew what went on in her own body, she knew how to control it – damn, damn, damn!

Her husband Mike was still training as a chartered surveyor but he was determined to support Cathy in whatever she wanted to do. He was equally aware that the decision had to be Cathy's alone if they were to avoid future recriminations. He did not want to be blamed as the cause of any eventual unhappiness.

Cathy went ahead with the pregnancy, determined to return to her career as soon as was physically possible, but her carefully laid plans were to suffer further knocks. Her son was born with a small deformity of the foot that required a series of operations before it was finally corrected. Cathy could not have predicted how devoted she was going to become as a mother and how her son's initial distress served to immeasurably strengthen the bond between them. Having remained at home for three years, she decided that she may as well complete her family and have a second child. This time it was a baby girl with no complications, but there was something wrong. Her inner self did not recognize as real the cosy domestic world she had created around her. She suffered from increasing bouts of depression. She had particular difficulty in relating to her daughter and this renewed the cycle of depression and guilt:

I felt completely lost in a colourless world from which there was no hope

29

of escape. I never felt desperate as extremes of feeling seemed futile. There just seemed to be no point to anything, including my relationship with my children.

Mike attached the convenient tag of postnatal depression to Cathy's condition and persuaded her to visit their GP. The doctor prescribed a short course of an antidepressant drug, but also urged her to consider talking to a therapist. This was the breakthrough. Through counselling Cathy finally managed to identify and understand the cause of her distress.

As the eldest daughter of the family Cathy had been fiercely ambitious and determined to 'prove' herself in terms of academic achievement. She subconsciously imagined that others were disappointed in her when she seemingly diverted from her aims by becoming a mother. Here she felt doubly confused because surely this was also what was expected of her by her parents. She still desperately sought their approval on the way she lived her life but felt literally torn in two by inner and outer pressures.

Enforced isolation at home, Mike's expectations of support from her and the blatant injustice of having no one to turn to herself, led to jealousy of him which soon turned to suppressed hostility. The birth of her daughter, with whose gender she identified, sparked off her depressive state because she felt she was herself caught in and was now replicating with her little girl an inescapable pattern. She had also lost her desire for contact with the outside world and the need to compete and succeed because she felt she was already defeated.

Once Cathy realized the root of her problem, she set about tackling it. She managed to get herself a part-time job with her old employers and Mike acted as a house husband while he was studying. This worked out well for both of them as Mike felt he was participating in 'parenting' and Cathy felt she had some support at last. She slowly regained her self-confidence and felt able to like herself again. She had finally achieved her ambition of successfully combining the internal world of the family and the external world of work.

The sudden enforced isolation that motherhood imposes can come as a tremendous emotional shock to a young woman in her twenties and can be the cause of much depression and anxiety. The transition from education and the support of an institution to work and self-sufficiency may be very recent. She has barely begun her trial period in the outside world when she is snatched away by a screaming blob and locked up in the foundations of a new nuclear family. Physical, let alone emotional, rescue seems unlikely. The father isn't going to put his career on ice for a couple of years and since the demise of the extended family Granny is set at one remove or banished out of sight.

The only source of emotional rescue is in fact likely to be other women – other mothers, young and not so young, experienced veterans with a string of toddlers trailing the pushchair, terrified ingenues, rich mums, poor mums, happy mums, desperate mums – gathering in little knots of solidarity around the climbing frame in parks and municipal playgrounds the length and breadth of the country, sharing their woes and their joys in the ancient mysteries of motherhood. However, for some young women for whom, like Cathy, motherhood has triggered a genuine depressive state, the condition of women merely reinforces the feeling of desolation: 'What poor fools we are.'

Germaine Greer neatly summed up the young mother's dilemma nearly two decades ago in *The Female Eunuch*:

The wife is only significant *qua* wife when she is bearing and raising the small children, but the conditions under which she carries out this important work and the confusion which exists about the proper way to perform it, increase her isolation from her community.

How can we learn to survive the pressures of early parenthood successfully? It is very important to understand that things are not going to be the same afterwards, especially the way we feel inside. Giving birth marks a fundamental life-change but, as John Cobb points out in his famous book *Babyshock*:

On the credit side, you should also realize that the change is just one part, albeit a most dramatic part, of a whole process of personal growth which can produce a mature, self-sufficient and positive individual.

It's possible to avoid the down side, postnatal depression, loss of self-confidence and isolation, if we can be fully prepared to fight it with a positive plan of campaign. There are basic principles of self-protection which can work very well when we are at our most vulnerable.

31

There is no single cause of the multiple symptoms that go to make up the state known as postnatal depression. These vary from mild feelings of inadequacy and pessimism to irrational fear of illness (either afflicting ourselves or those around us). These are often founded on the physical sensations that accompany depressive and anxiety states such as 'pins and needles', palpitations, sweating or a racing pulse. These symptoms, not surprisingly, frighten us and it seems impossible to put them down to simple anxiety. This starts a vicious cycle, friends and family lose patience with our self-obsession which seems to them, and more importantly to us, to border on actual madness.

A number of factors make some women more prone to postnatal depression than others. These are not necessarily all psychological, although it seems that certain personality types such as perfectionists are more likely to suffer. The flux in hormone levels, a 'bad' birth or a difficult baby can equally well trigger off a cycle of depression. A reduced or less satisfying sex life, plus the shock of moving perhaps from a socially stimulating career to a sinkful of nappies, either singly or in combination, can sometimes induce a state of severe depression.

We all react to stress in different ways. A universal solution cannot exist but certain simple precautions can damp down the seismic upheavals of babyshock. Emotional support is paramount from whatever source we can conjure up; firstly from our partners, family and friends – then from any outside source such as a health visitor, National Childbirth Trust contacts and so on. Talking to second-time mothers is also a very useful way of finding out what to expect and reminding ourselves that we are not alone in our experience.

Feeling that we are in charge of our immediate situation is vital, such as being able to make informed decisions on the manner of the delivery, where and how, and on the day-to-day routine of our new lives when the baby is born. Learning to delegate is a useful business skill that can be successfully applied to domestic life, for the simple and essential purpose of giving us at least some precious time alone.

The feelings of isolation and low self-worth described earlier can be diminished by keeping up as many of our pre-motherhood interests as is feasible and by maintaining some sort of social life. Seeing a good friend is often a far safer and more effective prescription against depression than a course of mind-numbing drugs.

Prolonged periods of isolation combined with stress, loud noise, uncertainty and dislocation of time is a classic brain-washing technique and that in various combinations is exactly what the arrival of a new baby brings. No wonder then that new mothers provde dangerously fertile ground for all sorts of phobias and acute panic attacks. One of the most pernicious of these is agrophobia, an inability to face the outside world at all.

AGORAPHOBIA

As we have seen, a woman in her early twenties may consciously or unconsciously choose marriage and babies rather than try and make it in the competitive and hostile world outside. Paradoxically, perhaps, the women most prone to suffer from the consequences of being 'stuck at home' are the very ones who may have chosen it in the first place as a means of escape. The onset of agoraphobia can rapidly transform 'home' into a terrifying prison. An initial attack can come quite suddenly and from then on the fear of another attack can confine the sufferer to familiar and apparently safe boundaries until they become impossible to cross. A sufferer may fear that if she goes outside the house she will lose the parameters that prescribe her existence and hence she will lose herself.

Christine, at the age of twenty-five, felt her life was over. Her agoraphobia had begun following the birth of her third child and, because she found it difficult and distressing to talk about her condition, even to her doctor, it gradually worsened until she was at last forced into the admission that she could not leave the house:

The thought of going to the supermarket filled me with horror. My hands would become wet with sweat, my heart pounding and pulse racing until I felt I was going to faint.

The degree of fear experienced by agoraphobics should not be

33

underestimated. Sensations of 'drowning', 'disappearing' or dying' are all common. Christine felt as bad as this but she could not confide in her doctor because she did not want to admit to what she saw as her own weakness, nor did she want to be treated with anti-anxiety drugs. Luckily for her, Christine's GP was finally able to reassure her that he believed she could overcome her problem by herself and that any drugs prescribed would only be a short-term way of getting through the immediate crisis. What he did give her were some simple exercises for controlling the panic at the onset of an attack (see pp. 126-8) and gradually Christine was able to recognize the warning signs of an oncoming attack and to deal with her symptoms as they arose. There was no overnight cure, it would have been unrealistic to expect it, but the fact that Christine had persevered and conquered her enemy virtually single-handed added to her own self-esteem and contributed to the rebuilding of her lost self-confidence.

Love, liberty and the pursuit of happiness

No matter what life-pattern emerges in our twenties – concentrating on a career while postponing committed partnerships and parenthood, or devoting ourselves entirely to marriage and motherhood – there is still a sense that we are doing what we feel compelled to do rather than what we really want. Our decisions appear to be informed ones (we're intelligent people, we read books and see films – we've seen our parents get it wrong or maybe even get it right) but lack of *real* life-experience lets us down. We are too often compelled to follow the line of least resistance and conform to the patterns of our parents or peer group. Leftover adolescent storms and tantrums still persist, the desire for personal freedom and a rebellious challenging of the 'system' sit uncomfortably alongside an urge to mate, settle down, get a mortgage, find our feet on an ambitious career ladder and so on. We feel we have to make our choices speedily and cannot conceive that any development of our personality in the future could cause us to deviate from the path we are on right now.

We have looked at the pressures and the potential dangers that threaten the emotional health of the stay-at-home mother in her twenties, but sometimes the single woman's will to succeed can also stand between her and the pursuit of happiness.

Kate is a vivacious twenty-five-year-old with a good job in a booming advertising agency. She pays lip-service to her personal freedom by boasting that she 'would never let the job interfere with my social life. I keep everything neatly compartmentalized – men, friends, family, work – are never allowed to overlap'. However, her increasing dependence on drink and cigarettes gives the lie to her neatly sorted and filed existence. She could not understand why she kept bursting into tears when she got home in the evening and had started to drink heavily on her own as a way of blotting out the tension she felt building up inside her. There was no obvious source of outside pressure, other than a rough and tough job, but she could handle that. Why did she feel she was on the verge of cracking up?

After confiding in a close friend, Kate reluctantly began attending a women's workshop which involved group therapy. Despite her initial scepticism, she became increasingly aware of the changes in her self-perception since she started to go to the weekly meetings:

When I first started going I thought I had got everything worked out very neatly and that there was just one minor adjustment to be made that would remove the pain and complete the perfect picture of how I wanted my life to be. Gradually I came to realize that all I had done was to split myself into pieces. Talking to other women who were going through similar experiences enabled me to start learning to accept myself the way I was rather than what I should be.

Getting involved in group therapy necessitates being your real self, something which many women, particularly in their self-conscious, role-playing twenties, are deeply frightened of. It means taking the risk of exposing our vulnerable inner self to the scrutiny of strangers, without any outer shell to protect us. The psychologist Carl Rogers who has spent thirty-five years studying and participating in group therapy sums up the experience thus: 'To discover that a whole group of people finds it much easier to care for the real self rather than for the facade is always a moving experience, not only for the person themselves but for the other members of the group as well'. This is how it worked for Kate.

Through group discussions Kate was able to start to interpret and understand the pressure building up inside her. Her family were all 'high achievers', her father was an architect, her brother a writer and her elder sister already ran her own successful PR company. Although it was never mentioned, Kate felt the onus was on her to fulfil family expectations, so she drove herself at work to the detriment not only of her relationships with men but also with other women. She wrote:

I sometimes felt that my time was so precious that not a minute must be wasted in which I could be furthering my ambitions. I rarely listened properly to what others were saying although I instinctively flirted with men when I thought it would do me some good. Sex was just another means to the same end, that of reaching some unattainable goal. Women I largely ignored altogether, unless they were successful in their careers, in which case I studied them to try and pick up tips on how it was done.

Her one close friendship dated from childhood and it was to this woman, Diana, that Kate finally turned for advice when her drinking began to get out of hand. Diana had been a member of a woman's group for some time and felt sure that Kate would benefit by letting down some of the barriers she had built around herself. Kate says now that through discussion and facing up to her feelings she discovered an unconscious conviction in herself that women were weak and ineffective and that, if she did not fight all that much harder, she would end up like her mother who she felt had 'wasted her life looking after everyone else'. Allowing people to come close seemed to invite a similar pattern of subjection and exploitation. Thus Kate shut out other people but as she herself recognized: 'What I did not realize was how much I needed to relieve my awful loneliness'.

Kate still has problems to work through with her mother but at least she feels she is now in touch with her real self and heading back in the right direction. She has changed her approach to life and in consequence her behaviour towards other people, while the unhappiness which prompted her to seek help in the first place has begun to resolve itself. She thinks she will eventually change her career too, as she now finds advertising less and less satisfying.

Realization of having made the 'wrong' choices in our twenties does not always require an immediate change in our circumstances. Continuing to consolidate a career or bring up and add to a young family may make more sense until we are sure of the next step and feel ready to take it. An awareness of what is wrong is enough to enable emotional growth to take place even when we can't do very much straightaway with our new-found maturity.

A young mother may well feel frustrated and hemmed in by her situation, but she wouldn't want to abandon her children even if she could. A successful career woman may long for a baby, but she can't go out and just acquire one as she might a word processor, grafting it on to her life as an optional extra. Both women may fully understand why they are unhappy but that realization will not instantly alleviate their distress. That understanding, however, may help them to accept the present by allowing them to start preparing for the future. That alone may be enough to restore their sense of control over their own destinies.

Taking risks in ways which might affect our external circumstances can be deferred until the time is right. Opening ourselves up to the possibility of internal change is what really counts. We may sometimes feel that everything in our lives is fixed by the time we hit twenty-nine, but for most of us the big three-o still signals a watershed and a time for a major self-appraisal.

The attitudes we held with such conviction in our twenties fall away. In their place is something else, an amorphous, free-floating anxiety. We can feel it physically, mentally and emotionally. Reluctant as we may be to admit, we recognize our foe in the ticking of our hormonal clock and beyond that our own mortality. This simple truth impels us in new directions during the decade that is to come. It is time for the main protaganist to take the centre stage.

3

High achievement, high anxiety: the thirties

Without doubt the period of maximum pressure, the toughest decade in a woman's life, is going to be the years that lie between young adulthood and midlife, the thirties. Whatever we want to do is circumscribed by the feeling, however vaguely felt, that there has to be a better life-plan than the one we have been working out in our twenties. As we boldly and inexorably voyage towards midlife, a myriad new pressures and responsibilities crowd in, while the decisions we may have put off in our twenties will wait for resolution no longer. Like grumpy out-patients sitting in a doctor's waiting room, they all line up demanding instant attention.

The loveless marriage which we may have made tolerable by channelling energies into a career or into children, can be endured no longer. Half-measures are no longer enough.

The single woman starts seeking a soulmate or, like the mechanically contraceiving couple, looks for a way of incorporating motherhood into her plans. For the woman who already has children there is the question of going back to work, having another baby or even combining both.

Divorce

Ten years of mediocre marriage and three children later, the hitherto philosophical and easy-going Helen plunged headlong into a desperate affair with the husband of her best friend. She believed it to be the 'real thing' and, after announcing her departure to a shellshocked husband, waited patiently for her lover to make the running and sweep her off to a new life.

Faced with an ultimatum from his wife, he voted with his feet for hearth and home and failed to deliver his side of the lover's pact. Helen was forced to take stock:

My husband still wanted me back but I knew things could not return to the way they were ever again. I had changed, or perhaps become aware of what I had really been all along. Whatever was to happen, I knew I had to make a complete break with my past if I was going to construct any sort of future for myself.

While sorting out the details of their divorce both Helen and her husband realized they were being more honest and showing more respect for one another than they had done in ten years of marriage. By now, however, it was too late:

Had we been able to communicate before, I don't believe things needed to have broken down. But once they had, it was too late to salvage much from the wreckage.

Helen claims that her divorce marked her transition to maturity, but the pull towards a return to 'stability', in the form of another attachment and renewed dependency on a man, was strong in spite of her revelling in her new-found autonomy. In less than a year she was living with and had a child by another man. She is determined not to let this relationship deteriorate in the way her marriage did and continues to believe in the viability of marriage, but she also acknowledges some feeling of regret and a sense of loss for her brief period of 'going solo':

After we sold the house, we split the profit and I bought a tiny two-up two-down in need of a lot of tender loving care. There was no central heating and there were great gaps in the walls where the plaster had crumbled away.

I had lost my husband, my lover and my best friend in one go. I had no visible means of support. I knew that my suffering, and by implication the children's, was entirely self-imposed. Yet sometimes I think I was happier alone in that hovel of a house than I had been before or since.

She supported herself successfully during this period by running a small, professional catering service, realizing in the process for the first time that she really was capable of self-reliance:

That gave me a tremendous boost. I felt powerful and sexy. Men also seemed to be drawn towards the new me. I was suddenly so popular that I was having to turn down invitations.

Paradoxically as soon as she settled down again, her newly-discovered allure rapidly disappeared. Although Helen now describes herself as 'contented', her brief radiance has been eclipsed once more by the return of her emotional and economic dependence on a man.

Statistically the early to mid-thirties are the peak age for discontented couples to slouch dolefully towards the courtroom. Whether or not divorce marks any kind of passage towards emotional development of course depends entirely on individual circumstances but, whatever the divorce is ending, it is also the beginning of something else. Whatever sadness lies in the past, the future can be seen full of promise – a new career, new relationships, new possibilities for love.

However, divorce alone is not a key to new-found happiness. Even if it is inevitable, it still remains a bereavement which requires mourning. We cannot discard a marriage like an old dress, it must be accepted as having had a place in our lives, however unhappy we may have been at the time. Erasing it completely is impossible and trying to suppress the mixed feelings of guilt and sorrow for its failure is just storing up trouble for the future.

This powerful cocktail of emotions will be common to both parties in a divorce; shock, hostility, depression, guilt and relief may jostle as uncomfortably in the mind of the transgressor as the transgressed. Unless these feelings are worked through, they can easily taint future hopes of happiness. Retrospective jealousies and old hurts lie dormant but they are capable of stunting any new relationship.

The aspects of life that bind a couple to one another, as well as serving to reinforce their separate existence, are all shattered at one blow. It is often difficult to take in the significance of this change. Children, home, parental and individual roles are all rearranged, like some grim, grown-up game of musical chairs.

Every aspect of their previous lives, down to the last detail, is suddenly different. There may well be an overwhelming sense of failure, resulting in feelings of regret and anxiety. The finality of the loss may not be accepted for some time by the one who has been left, who may harbour secret hopes of reconciliation.

Letting go of a live traitor is sometimes more difficult than accepting the death of a beloved partner. Ironically, for some couples it can be the complete absence of love that forms the bounds of reality. Some women come to rely on the turbulence of a failing relationship, poisonous and corrosive as it may be, to supply a staple of emotional stimulus, just as much if not more than the prospect of enduring love. The divorce itself, with its attendant acrimony and the sudden, highly-public apportioning of blame, can be the subconsciously-sought grand operatic climax of this process, an emotional feast at the time but one which leaves a hangover of bitter emptiness.

RECONCILIATION COUNSELLING

Counselling is designed to screen out as much acrimony and unhappiness as possible from troubled marriages and minimize the potential emotional damage to any children involved. Both partners are given a chance to explore and untangle their confused emotions and to avoid simply putting the blame on to one or another. With one in three marriages now ending in divorce and the failure rate of second marriages getting even greater, the value of providing this kind of emotional support for every member of a family where the marriage is breaking down is being recognized on a wider level. The Family Courts Service helps separating couples to decide what they want, in terms of access to or custody of their children, before coming to court. This enables them to sort out their differences on neutral ground, and prevents the build-up of bitterness that may stem from the poisonous mixture of legal and emotional wrangling in open court. Research has shown that such long-drawn-out hostilities can have a devastating effect on the future emotional security and happiness of the children. The staff of the Family

Courts Service tend to be experienced social workers with experience of working with families in the divorce and domestic courts (it is a statutory body, so the service is free to any family that needs it).

Children, so often the innocent victims of divorce, are frequently bewildered by what's happening and interpret it as being in some way their fault. They feel that their bad behaviour is responsible for the separation and that the parent who has left no longer loves them. They are in need of a great deal of emotional support, and reassurance of both parents' continuing affection, if they are to survive the experience unscarred.

This can place an intolerable burden on the parent who is primarily responsible for the children (and in most cases that means their mother) as it falls on her to help the children to cope just when her own resources are at their lowest ebb. Here professional counselling from a marriage guidance counsellor as well as the support of friends and family can provide a valuable backup. It is very important to explain fully to the children exactly what is going on and make sure they have no false illusions about a family reconciliation. A counsellor can help a parent through this time and also contribute in the process of conciliation so that both parents realize the importance of containing their bitterness against one another in the best interests of their children. It may take some considerable time before a deserted spouse feels ready to face the world alone again. Meanwhile many people feel the need to come back to such sessions to talk through their feelings *after* the trauma of divorce has been worked through. Three divorce conciliators with great experience of the distress caused by family breakdown are Chris Hawkes, John Howard and Jo Morello. They describe some of their findings in their book *Divorce, Children and Separation*:

If what we have observed is anything to go by, then in England alone there must be many thousands of people, employees, self-employed whatever, whose marriage divorce and emotional problems are acute enough to distract them seriously from their daily work. Productivity and performance suffers as days are taken off to 'sort a few things out', or to 'get some tablets from the doctor to help me sleep', or simply because they cannot face a day's concentration.

43

In the majority of divorce cases, custody of the children is granted to the woman. However, in the turmoil of a bust-up and in the voyage through the legal aftermath, getting custody may well be the only clearly defined aim, while all else for the time being is confusion. Of course, success in getting the children places enormous pressure upon a suddenly isolated single parent coping with an entirely new financial, let alone emotional, environment. In Britain in the late eighties one in eight family households have single parents, the great majority women.

For some a failed marriage is the sad but inevitable consequence of an alliance that was ill matched from the beginning. Just walk away and start again. For others it is a tragic squandering of human potential and happiness, felt all the more keenly because of the ability to step outside and see how mutually destructive they are being, but how powerless they are to stop themselves. Loss of communication is a frequently cited cause of 'irretrievable breakdown' and is often the fatal flaw in the marital drama. Once the emotional barricades have been piled high, inside the fortress there is nowhere new to go. This introspective retreat and self-imposed isolation merely camouflages hostility which would otherwise be expressed (and maybe in the process harmlessly released like steam from a safety valve). Unable to find an outlet in open battle, the internal conflict can sometimes become a sexual one.

Psychosexual problems

Wherever women get together these days, talk of sex, good, bad or otherwise comes unselfconsciously. The old order is changing, but women, traditionally the nurturers and self-blamers, are still far more likely to acknowledge and seek assistance with emotional difficulties than men and will often, too often, take responsibility for something which is their lover's problem.

Sue is a thirty-four-year-old fashion buyer with two children of eight and ten. Although married for twelve years to Tom, an oil executive, she recounts how difficult it was for her to discuss sex with him:

Neither of us could ever seem to find the right words. I was always wary of sounding critical of what he regarded as his 'performance'. I didn't want to dent the macho image he had of himself, because I sensed how vulnerable he was beneath the façade.

Like so many women, Sue's reluctance to explore or express her own needs at the threatened expense of Tom's ego resulted in their suppression. This in turn engendered a series of psychosomatic disorders.

Persistent pain on the right-hand side of her abdomen led to hospital investigations for suspected appendicitis on several occasions. Sue also complained constantly of fatigue and loss of enjoyment of life generally. Diagnoses ranged from possible pelvic inflammatory disease to clinical depression. Feeling, quite naturally, that no one was really helping her, Sue began to become an increasingly withdrawn and difficult patient.

Sue was lucky in having a GP who finally took the initiative himself. She had almost become a permanent resident in his surgery. Her friends and family were mystified as to what could have transformed such a happy and outgoing young woman into such a depressed and silent wraith, and they were fast losing sympathy. Luckily, Sue's doctor looked further than her physical symptoms and, rather than start prescribing tranquilizers, encouraged her to talk confidentially. Slowly and agonizingly it emerged that Sue had not enjoyed sex for several years but was totally incapable of communicating this to her husband, who was becoming as edgy and depressed as she was. She had tried to get through often enough but, weighed down by the pressures of work, Tom had ignored her distress signals.

Sue had interpreted her resentment through her body by developing psychosomatic complaints so convincing that she could easily, had she had a less sensitive GP, have been referred for surgery.

Her GP persuaded Sue to bring Tom to the surgery with her and encouraged them to talk things through together. They both found the presence of a trusted 'outsider' helped to create a calm atmosphere where they felt safe to discuss their intimate feelings without the anxiety or tension they had come to associate with home. As Tom began to realize that, his very real concern and affection for Sue showed through. This reassurance gave Sue the confidence she had been lacking to tell Tom frankly how she felt about their sex life without fearing his hostility. Happily, they are able to look back and even laugh at this potential traumatic episode, but for thousands of other women a story like this could involve tranquillizers or alcohol dependency, unnecessary surgery, depression or divorce.

Often the marital incompatibility that first brings a couple to their GP is not a sexual one. It may well be the secondary results of disagreements over money, relatives, children, job pressures and so on. If this is the case and the doctor feels that the couple require more than just a sympathetic talk he will most likely refer them to a Marriage Guidance Council (MGC) sexual dysfunction clinic or to a psychosexual therapist through the Association of Sexual and Marital Therapists.

Having recognized the problem as a sexual one – the first cause and not the effect of disharmony – and taken the first step towards getting help, what actually happens at the first interview with a counsellor? Initially the counsellor meets with a couple both separately and together to determine whether this kind of therapy will be beneficial. A couple do not have to be married but must be part of an apparently continuing and caring relationship. MGC counsellors do not see couples who want to come specifically to conceive a child, and couples are asked to practice contraception until the therapy sessions have ended. This is quite simply because pregnancy can cause increased or decreased desire in a woman and may mask the basic sexual difficulty.

At the initial interview the couple and their counsellor must decide whether they like one another and feel they can work together. There must be this kind of rapport for there to be any chance of success. After this joint interview the couple are seen separately for what is called history-taking.

History-taking involves recording early sex experience, the

46

kind of affection shown within the client's family, and family attitudes towards sex – anything in fact which may have influenced their personal attitude towards sex, its importance within their marriage and their respect for their partner.

If the counsellor discovers that either one of the partners is having an affair, they ask the partner to be honest about it. They feel that the therapy cannot be successful if there is not absolute honesty on both sides.

Also, if there is no sexual difficulty in the extramarital affair it might well indicate that the trouble is lack of love rather than any sexual dysfunction. After the separation for history-taking the couple and the counsellor meet again for a joint discussion, to decide whether sexual therapy would be helpful for them. If they all (including the counsellor) agree that it would, a series of weekly sessions is arranged. What happens at these sessions depends on the nature of the problem. The most common difficulties encountered are vaginismus (involuntary tightening of vaginal muscles to prevent penetration), inability to sustain an erection, premature ejaculation, or lack of orgasm.

By far the greatest single cause of any of these so called 'dysfunctions' is emotional distress. Physical factors account for a very small proportion of cases. 'Sexual dysfunction' sounds a clinically cold label for the body's temporary inability to respond in the way we would like. This can be due to a great variety of causes ranging from family taboos to the recollection, involuntary or otherwise, of some previous sexual episode involving fear or pain. Whatever the initial cause of a sexual problem, once it has begun it creates a vicious circle, generating fear of failure, which must be broken. One way of breaking into that circle is to encourage the couple to change their attitudes in regarding sex in terms of 'performance', and to concentrate on sharing pleasure at many different levels.

At each of these sessions couples are given 'tasks' such as a series of touching or stroking exercises to lead them gradually to the appreciation of joint physical pleasure combined with emotional fulfilment. This method is known as 'sensate focus' and was a standard technique of the pioneer sexologists Masters and Johnson. They may also be encouraged to experiment with, and to examine their attitude towards, previously unexplored sexual activities. The whole thing, to use a sixties cliché, is designed to put them 'in touch with their feelings', but there is nothing clichéd about the results. Previously immovable blocks between couples have been shifted by this method far more effectively than by using words alone.

As in Sue and Tom's case, in matters of sex words can sometimes be more of a barrier than a facilitator of communication. In spite of living today against a cultural background of sexual openness, speaking frankly and fully about individual sexual needs, of personal likes and dislikes, remains painfully difficult for some people. Nobody would criticize an individual for being shy about sex but where two people are interacting, misunderstanding one another's actions leads to problems.

Shyness seems like lack of enthusiasm, soon to be interpreted as lack of love, whereas passion appears as selfish lust. A counsellor can do much to defuse such resentments by encouraging a couple to talk in simple terms about their likes and dislikes. They will often find they have been getting each other quite wrong. If people have never talked about sex before it is sometimes a great relief to discover that they are not alone in experiencing sexual problems. They may well have been imagining themselves to be freaks if, for example, they fail to achieve orgasm.

Parental, cultural and religious pressures have all had their part to play in influencing our sexual attitudes. When there is a conflict between this deeply ingrained personal programming and the temptation to step over its boundaries, the conflict can show up as sexual dysfunction. The psychosexual counsellor can begin to untie these emotional knots by giving clients 'permission' to shed their taboos, to discover their bodies and their sexual possibilities without shame.

Sex is only one component of a couple's relationship, but it is a powerful means of expressing other emotions, other feelings and judgements about one another, good or bad. One partner's need to subdue can show up as a demanding, dominating attitude towards sex. Criticism of passivity can reflect a general resentment about lack of ambition or earning power – sex is always much more about what's going on between two people than the act of intercourse.

'Performance', in terms of male erection and ability to control ejaculation, and a woman's ability to reach orgasm, is obviously important in a mechanistic sense but not as much as the deeper feelings of desire, arousal, tenderness and intimacy. Without fulfilment of these in some measure the whole episode becomes mere physical release – 'putting the jam in the doughnut', as Ms Greer once graphically described it.

By far the most common sexual problem for women is vaginismus. However much a woman may desire intercourse she cannot relax her involuntarily tensed vaginal muscles to allow penetration – it looks like rejection of the male partner in the most embarrassingly forceful way, a simple sexual dysfunction which leads straightaway to emotional distress in both partners.

The case history of a couple who sought help (in the first instance for 'infertility') illustrates how deep this distress can be. Diana is a thirty-five-year-old management consultant. Half Italian by birth, she had been brought up as a strict, convent-educated Catholic. She seemed attractive, warm, friendly, not at all 'cold' or 'prudish' in any sense, a modern woman who apparently had reconciled the faith of her childhood to her grown-up self; but after thirteen years of marriage Diana was a virgin. She was completely unable to let her husband Colin enter her although she claimed to love him, she even encouraged him to seek physical gratification elsewhere (although he had never done so). She believed the birth of a child through artificial insemination would solve their problem.

In the course of counselling it emerged that Diana could not resolve the ambivalence of her Catholic teaching on sex before and after marriage:

The wedding ceremony seemed such a farce. Suddenly I had to reverse all my previous attitudes towards physical intimacy. Having held myself in check for so long, I no longer knew how to respond naturally.

This was the first time Diana had ever felt able to discuss these suppressed feelings so openly. There was no immediate

49

miraculous improvement in their sex life, but a gradual and slow progress as they became used to talking to one another both about their intimate feelings and sex itself. Diana realized she had been treating her husband as an intruder in every sense, a stranger invading her body. Once she could allow herself to accept him as a lover and a friend she was able to relax and let him cross both her psychological and physical boundaries.

Dr Rosalie Taylor, a psychosexual therapist with many years of experience, places importance on individual therapy and on maintaining a flexible approach to treatment:

It may be important to examine the patient physically, particularly a woman in whom much of the sexual apparatus is so hidden and mysterious that she can feel very divorced from it. But the examination must not be intrusive, and the physician must have deep respect for her feelings as this helps her to feel the possessor of her own body and to be aware of its goodness.

Sex therapy is not a remedy for all ills nor are all minor health problems psychosexual. Of course there are many causes of marriages breaking down other than sex and sexual dysfunction. Even when the problem is primarily sexual, for some people therapy may not always be the answer; but for many others who are enduring unnecessarily joyless partnerships it can help to find a way of communicating again, a chance for happiness through good sex.

Remaking families and the challenge of step-parenting

Divorce is not just about endings – it can be about beginnings, about new chances for happiness, new children, new families. It's also very often about remaking families out of the broken bits of what's been before. This can be one of the most emotionally demanding of all jobs women are called on to perform at any time in their lives.

Both Valerie and her husband Alan, a forty-year-old sales executive, have two teenage children apiece from former marriages. Valerie is the main buffer between these two tribes. Her invalid mother has just come to live with the already extended family at the same time that Alan's elderly father has been diagnosed as suffering from cancer of the throat. Although Alan was reluctant to put any more pressure on Valerie, he could not face the idea of dumping his father in a nursing home for his last few months of life.

Valerie herself was torn between picking up her career and having a last and much longed-for baby, both for herself and for Alan. The internal pressure was building as the external pressure was becoming insupportable.

How did Valerie survive this emotional onslaught without buckling? She was a practical woman. She was a trained manager. She determined to face up to realities and do the best she could in the circumstances, a perfect solution was out of reach so something less than perfect would have to do.

Luckily Alan was anxious to help relieve the pressure in any way that he could and they sat down to discuss what was in effect a plan of war:

I was determined to win. If you want something strongly enough it's amazing what hidden resources you can summon to your aid. And I did want it all, the late baby, a career of my own, a loving relationship with my mother and father-in-law.

Together Alan and Valerie talked to the teenagers and coaxed a non-aggression pact and a treaty of cooperation out of them, creating the right conditions for Valerie to wage her campaign. Both sets of adolescents turned out to be surprisingly willing to help, impressed at Valerie's valiant tackling of the challenges in front of her. Alan's daughter Sophie, who at the age of seventeen was a keenly analytical feminist, went so far as to suggest that Alan became a fulltime househusband. Luckily, Valerie had always had a good relationship with both her stepchildren, whose natural mother had died when they were still at primary school. Sophie's younger brother Mark summed up her success:

She never tried to 'replace' our mother. Other friends of mine have stepmothers who seem phoney. They want to be 'first' mother and friend all at once and it doesn't work. They end up being resented all round.

It seems that knowing who you are and establishing that identity within the new family is an important first step towards gaining respect. Valerie had achieved this vital foothold, so when it came to calling for assistance she found herself surrounded by willing helpers.

Not that there hadn't been early strains. Valerie recalled lost weekends of physical and emotional exhaustion as Alan played nonstop stand-up comedian trying, she supposed, to win over her own sons, Richard and James. Not only did they give him the bird, she began asking herself how she had ever come to marry this tedious buffoon:

It was so wearing. I found that by Sunday night my face was frozen rigid in a strychnine smile. But underneath I knew why he was doing it. As tactfully as possible in the circumstances I told him just to be himself if he wanted the boys to accept him. His relief at not having to perform any more was far funnier than his act had ever been.

Being a step-parent is not easy. There is no quick path through the emotional minefield of everyone's feelings on such sensitive issues as ex-spouses, discipline, resentment, sex and lingering guilt. Realizing these potential pitfalls in advance is the way to survive step-parenthood. With more than five million second families in the UK alone the issues of step-parenthood are becoming more and more relevant to an ever-growing number of people, most of whom are in the thirty to forty age group.

A stepfamily can be as strong and viable as a conventional family but its strengths and vulnerabilities are not the same and it is better for everyone both in and outside the relationship not to pretend that it is. We cannot expect immediate and perfect love from our recently-acquired family. A step-child's affection must be won, something which can prove as emotionally gruelling as any unrequited love affair. It's a highly complex situation for both a child and an adult, otherwise complete strangers, to form bonds that take years to grow anyway in an 'ordinary' family.

Another big emotional problem is the ex-wife. She can seem a loomingly powerful figure, an 'ever-present ghost' haunting the new relationship. A periodic phone call or meeting can serve to exorcise some of the fear, guilt and hurt on both sides but it's probably wisest to lay off discussing the shared man and the days when he was hers, not yours.

As in Valerie and Alan's case, it pays to treat the children as sentient beings. Consulting them beforehand so they have a chance to get used to the idea of a new step-parent is going to be a wise move. It is not permission-seeking so much as evidence of your loving concern for their happiness in the future together. Remember that the simple fact of proximity and the length of time spent in each other's company results in far more strain for the stepmother than the stepfather. Even in a straightforward nuclear family, the father can often be a more popular figure than the mother, who has perforce to maintain domestic order.

In the middle of all this worrying over stepchildren, making sure the adults get sufficient time together is vitally important and privacy must be jealously guarded. The kind of problems caused by poor communication are likely to pose more of a threat in relationships where it is difficult to find time alone together. Letting the children know that there are set limits on their intrusion into their parents' lives is important for everyone.

Obviously there are many, many problems – not just emotional ones – involved in step-parenting but there is a good side, not the least being the satisfaction of forming a relationship with a child who is not one's own and being accepted as that child's role-model for his or her attitudes to partnerships and togetherness.

Since Alan was self-employed his working hours were flexible. Together the six of them were able to work out a routine whereby there would nearly always be someone in the house. Costing out the exercise showed that even with Valerie's new salary they would not be able to afford nursing care for both parents and help with the baby. Help came from their GP who, accustomed as he was to seeing elderly relatives despatched to the nearest nursing home, was impressed by Valerie's courage and compassion. He arranged daily nursing-home visits for both parents, meaning they could just afford a mother's help when the baby was born.

A year later Valerie had a baby daughter, Charlotte, much cossetted by the whole family. Alan's father died just before she was born so the pregnancy was by no means easy for Valerie – but in spite of everything she remains proud of this domestic victory, not just for herself but for the whole family.

Talking to Valerie and others like her it becomes clear just what an enormous undertaking it is to refire, let alone strive to fulfil, ambitions which have been suppressed since a woman's early twenties. Betty Friedan illustrates the plight of the 'deferred achiever' with the memorable comment: 'It was easier for me to start the women's movement than to change my own personal life'.

Part of the problem is often the haziness of our own goals. Ambition does not wither while women are busy having babies and bringing up families; it waits to flower again, but once the family has grown it becomes difficult to remember who we were in that distant time when we were young adults with no dependants. Having grown used to denying our own needs, in some women's cases to the point of self-immolation, of course it is hard to redefine a role for ourselves that includes self-gratification, that allows our needs and wants to come first. If we cannot find a way through, ambitious energies which need to be directed to the outside world beyond the family will turn inwards on it and ourselves, with destructive results.

In the eighties, when feminism has to some extent helped to define motherhood as a temporary phase, these unfulfilled ambitions can hurt even more, but feminism has also provided something positive to hang on to in the stream of role-models and operating assumptions for those deferred achievers anxious to get back to concerns away from the family. That's what's expected. That's what everybody seems to be doing. That's the point where Yuppy culture, with its work ethic allied with a ruthless, glossy magazine acquisitiveness, meets the fustier feminism of the *Guardian's* Women's Page. However, there is a danger that this 'new' culture of the successful woman may cause some women to transfer guilt for failing as a nurturer to guilt for failing as an achiever.

Either way, the tug between home and work, between the needs of the family and the needs of ourselves feeling our way back into the outside world, can cause tremendous strains

—which, ironically, show up as emotional distress at the time when the family doesn't need the nurturer any more. Many women with families growing up approach the forties with the feeling, what the hell do I do now? Forty years more with the food processor suddenly doesn't seem that attractive.

In comparison to the deferred achiever, life seems fairly straightforward for the achiever who has deferred a family. However, appearances are often deceptive. Having postponed maternity until after the portentous age of thirty, some women may find that the primal urge to reproduce can begin to fade, or at least be intellectuallized away. Often it's a case of too many other things happening instead—career, lovers, money, success and a pattern of life into which the intrusion of a squashed tomato in a Babygrow would seem as absurd as inviting a chimpanzee round for tea.

The biological clock

At the age of thirty-seven Jan found she had spent ten years deliberating half seriously about children without coming to any conclusion:

I envied the sister-in-law I used to pity. Carol had got pregnant accidentally ten years ago, on her honeymoon. It was twins and the shock was overwhelming but she coped well and brought up two beautiful children. The decision was taken out of her hands. With modern methods of contraception, of course, there is only a small chance of having it happen to you. David my husband says he has no strong feelings either way and that it's up to me. I always end up thinking of all the nice things, holidays, meals out and so on we would have to miss out on. I also wonder about my patience with a small child and whether I could cope now. I know I am being selfish but I am a realist. Deep down I don't know whether I want our life to change to that extent.

Meanwhile, as her biological clock ticks on, the likelihood of Jan conceiving a child recedes, but the emotional anguish does not. From the age of thirty-five onwards, awareness grows that whatever the rest of our life may hold, and it may hold a lot, we can only seek to put our own children into the pattern within a few precious and fleeting years. It is not just childless women who may feel like this. Mothers are often tempted into 'one last pregnancy', sometimes for the joy of it, sometimes as an excuse for further postponement of any return to the world outside the family. Sometimes a woman whose life seems immaculately organized, with her family growing up, a career about to be re-established, will have a mysterious and self-immolating conception, the final decision about the pattern of her life being made by default.

Does the experience of a late baby differ from motherhood in the twenties? Joanna, a veteran at thirty-nine with twin thirteen-year-old boys and an eighteen-month-old girl from a second marriage, is delighted at the confirmation of her pregnancy:

I am far less selfish now than I was at twenty-five. When the boys were small it is sad but true that I was completely self-occupied with myself and the state of my unhappy marriage. Nick and I are now so happy that I can feel free to devote all my time to enjoying these two latecomers. Fortunately, my two older sons, William and Tom, are besotted by their new sister Sarah. I think the fact she is a different sex from them stops her from posing a threat. But I also try to involve them as much as possible because I am aware of feeling guilt about them.

Of course, in physical terms Joanna knows what to expect from a new baby – broken nights and frantic days – but how does such an experience hit the 'deferred nurturer'?

Anna, a journalist on a national newspaper, decided to become pregnant at thirty-eight, even though it would mean a significant break in her career:

I hadn't thought about it for all that long. Being totally absorbed in my career up until then I had always felt I couldn't spare the time. But after thirty-five I found my attitudes changing. My priorities altered, I wanted to slow down for a while and take stock, although there were moments when I was terrified that I might be putting an end to everything I had worked so hard for. In fact, the opposite was true. The baby has been a wonderful new beginning for me.

Anna thinks that being prepared for a radical change in lifestyle helps the late mother to survive the stresses. It may also carry the added bonus of a healthier living pattern for both mother and baby. After years of junk food, parties and working late, Anna found early nights (even if interrupted), regular meals and a big cut-down in smoking and drinking made her feel a lot healthier.

Pregnancy gave me the reason to make and keep all the resolutions I never had the will-power to carry through before.

Since the advent of amniocentesis, whereby foetal abnormalities such as Down's syndrome can be detected early in pregnancy by withdrawing a sample of amniotic fluid, even conception at forty-plus is no longer frowned upon by doctors. Pregnancy complications in older women have perhaps always been exaggerated, sometimes to suit the convenience of the medical profession, but medical innovations mean that labour complications arising from diabetes or hypertension can now be prevented or controlled.

Anna was fortunate in having a supportive and loving partner with whom to share both the emotional and physical strains as well as the unexpected pleasures of postponed parenthood, but what of those brave women without men, who deliberately decide to go it alone and apparently cold-bloodedly select the father of their child as others might the sire of their pedigree Siamese cat? It is not difficult to understand why unattached women over thirty whose fertility is on the wane do not feel they have many options open to them, and not so much time left for making up their mind.

Getting pregnant as the deliberate result of a one-night stand seems rather unsatisfactory. On the other hand, artificial insemination can seem too coldly clinical to some people. Quite a few women faced with this dilemma are putting a good deal of thought and time into selecting a biological father for their offspring, a potentially emotionally complex operation.

Thirty-seven-year-old Nicky is one such woman. She has spent the last two years considering her many male friends on the basis of their intellect, their health, looks and, as she put it, 'lack of emotional hang-ups'. Some men she approached were flattered but shied away from such a potentially dangerous relationship.

Other men felt that, however dispassionate they might feel about sex, even sex that led to a conception, the danger of emotional entanglements with mother and child were too great. They could hardly imagine themselves having no interest whatsoever in their offspring's future, perhaps they would want legal rights . . . this was getting complicated.

So Nicky decided to renegotiate her terms. She was obviously not going to find a prospective father willing to be discarded once conception had taken place and his usefulness was over. There was going to be more to this than just being in the right bed at the right time.

Then Steve, an ex-boyfriend from way back, suddenly resurfaced in her life. Independence of spirit had been the common factor that had drawn them together in the first place, then had eventually driven them apart. Each of them was touched and surprised to find the other still the same in spite of the years between, during which most of their contemporaries had settled into conformist, comfortable grooves. The next step was obvious.

Nicky got pregnant. Although she says that she and Steve have a very strong relationship based on deep mutual attraction and respect, they had found several attempts at living together cloying and destructive. They have proposed a workable if unusual life-pattern in which Steve will visit his child whenever he likes but has no 'formal' right of access. British law only recognizes fathers who are registered as such on the child's birth certificate. Steve is not. Both remain optimistic about their chances of developing an independent relationship with their child and think this will rule out any possible ill effects from being brought up in a one-parent family.

Friends with children conceived in more conventional circumstances remain sceptical although all wish Nicky well. They fear that Nicky does not and maybe cannot appreciate how tough looking after a baby can be, especially trying to work and earn at the same time. Nicky's mother worries about the stigma of illegitimacy. However, all are determined to provide her with whatever they can and not to show they feel Nicky is doing anything 'wrong'. Her choice is just another design from the increasingly complicated yet imaginative patternbook of women's lives.

Infertility, AID, adoption and adapting to childlessness

INFERTILITY

Perhaps that word 'choice' needs further definition. Many couples spend fifteen years of their lives or more doing everything to prevent conception, only to discover in their mid-thirties that they are suddenly being diagnosed as 'infertile'. Having that cruel label stuck on her is one of the most emotionally stressful experiences a woman can undergo. Paradoxically, it can strike just as hard at women who have never even considered having children as it can those who long for them. It threatens sexual identity and self-esteem. The biblical expression 'barren' conveys the depressing aridity that can threaten a partnership or personal self-worth.

The fear of infertility can also overshadow many relationships. Even when there is no physiological problem with either partner, getting pregnant can often take two years or more but persuading people that a perfectly planned-for baby cannot be engendered just like that gets tricky after a lot of trying and no apparent result. The treatment of infertility remains a severe emotional strain on any couple. The combined pressure of consultations, bloodtests, injections, possibly even surgery, allied to the uncertainty of the eventual outcome, make the whole process a very rough emotional ride.

Such strain can push a relationship in one of two ways. Some discover new depths of feeling for each other and can translate the experience into a consolidating one, but others fall prey to intense fears and anxieties and find themselves tearing at each other.

So how can we cope with such an emotional issue? Most religions teach that childlessness should be accepted passively, but an arrogant faith in medical science has encouraged us to believe that babies can be prevented or produced entirely at our

our own volition. It is often the achieving woman, used to making all the major decisions in her life, who feels it most strongly when she cannot fulfil the most fundamentally female function of them all, conceiving and bearing a child.

Why one should want a child is a feeling that defies simple analysis, yet is is a question that an infertile couple is continually asked by those who would seek to help them, including their family and friends. Why should one want a child? Do we do it out of overwhelming biological urgency, our selfish genes seeking to reproduce themselves down the generations? Is it something to do with replicating the ego and challenging mortality? Is it something to give to one's partner? Is it providing something to our parents? Whatever the reasons, however trivial, selfish, or heart-renderingly sincere the motivations, wanting a child and being unable to conceive one, can put a woman under enormous pressure. Facing up to a partner's infertility can be almost as painful as confronting one's own.

Finding ways around the problem (once medicine has done its utmost) must involve making sure that everyone's feelings are considered. When the urge for a child is getting irresistible, it is all too easy to grab at apparently straightforward solutions such as adoption or AID (Artificial Insemination by Donor) without pausing to consider the emotional issues that these apparently 'simple' answers are going to raise.

The discovery of infertility can represent as deep a shock as the death of a member of the family. The future can seem just as blighted. Time is needed to recover from the 'bereavement' before looking for an alternative method of 'producing' a child. Part of the problem is that there is no object for a grieving would-be-parent to focus upon. The sense of loss thus becomes a free-floating one which can quickly deteriorate into a more generalized and intractable state of depression.

Finding out you are infertile is not just a thirty-second drama conducted in the doctor's consulting room. For some people it is a painfully long process of fading hope and increasing fear. Anger, depression, resentment and jealousy of other people's children are all fairly common reactions.

Jealousy in particular can be a very destructive emotion,

isolating the sufferer from her family and friends and often making the situation worse.

ARTIFICIAL INSEMINATION BY DONOR (AID)

Julia, a thirty-four-year-old stylist, had been living with Phil, a freelance photographer, for twelve years before they decided to start a family. Neither of them had any worries whatsoever about their ability to conceive straightaway. Both came from large families and all Julia's sisters had several babies apiece. Phil had also built himself quite a reputation as a ladies' man during his bachelor days and suffered from a common male misapprehension that sexual prowess and fertility are inextricably linked (they are entirely unrelated).

After eighteen months of 'trying for a baby', both began to become dispirited to say the least. Each secretly began to blame the other. Rows became more frequent and Julia realized that it would be better to confront the real cause of their conflict. She asked Phil if he would mind undergoing infertility tests with her. His reaction was hostile, but after much nursing of hurt pride, he finally agreed to go.

Julia was asked to fill in a daily temperature chart to ensure she was ovulating properly, while Phil, much to his embarrassment, was asked to produce a semen sample for analysis. They were told that if the results of the tests proved normal, further investigations, such as examination of Julia's cervical mucus or an X-ray of her womb and Fallopian tubes to make sure there were no blockages, would be the next step.

None of this was necessary. Phil's sperm count (the number of sperm per cubic millilitre of seminal fluid) was far too low for any chance of conception. He was knocked sideways, and he looks back at that time as one of extreme stress:

I had a terrible problem coming to terms with my infertility for a long time but now I think that the experience taught me a lot too. I came to see that it had nothing to do with my virility and that I was still the same person I had always been. I was able to chuck out all that stupid macho philosophy of 'real' men being able to make babies, and concentrate instead on what was really important – my relationship with Julia. I started thinking about her instead and what I could do to

61

make her happy. What really helped me to work it all out was talking to the infertility counsellor.

Couples who go for infertility treatment are usually offered support counselling both before and after each stage of the investigations.

Both Julia and Phil now say that they realize they would just have drifted apart during this period of intense emotional stress without the backup of someone who had seen it all through before. Each of them feels that they went through a private hell but that they learned a lot about themselves in the process.

Julia now says that she was so distraught at the time that she couldn't bring herself to speak to Phil's sister when she rang to say that she was pregnant two days after they had received the news of Phil's sterility.

It sounds completely insane now but I couldn't bring myself to congratulate her. I even felt as though I wished his sister would lose it.

I didn't want to see other women. Even if they didn't actually have any children, I was aware all the time that they could if they wanted to. That was what started me thinking about artificial insemination. It was Phil, not me, who was infertile. I think that thought would have driven us apart if he had not been able to accept my having a child this way.

Julia never told Phil this at the time, since she felt it would have been unfair for him to feel that he was being forced into such a serious commitment against his will.

But we did discuss it for a long time first. I didn't have any adverse feelings about carrying another man's child inside me but I could see that it might be an unsurmountable problem for some women as well as a lot of men.

Initially Phil felt 'very peculiar' about the whole arrangement, but after talking to a counsellor and another couple they knew had conceived in this way, Phil began to feel that he could cope with the situation. They decided that they too would be completely open about Phil's sterility and the fact that Julia was receiving AID and that they would also try to be equally open with the child when it came along. They both felt that although it might be difficult to explain to a child what AID is all about, the effect of discovering the news during the turbulent teenage years could ultimately be far more disrupting. Being frank about the problems of infertility and receiving AID is also a good way of lessening the general lack of knowledge and possible prejudice that couples like Phil and Julia often encounter.

Phil's parents were worried that other people might notice their grandchild's lack of resemblance to their son and might make fun of him. In fact the selection of a donor is a very regulated procedure which includes the matching of hair and eye colouring as well as screening for possible hereditary problems. Phil and Julia are now the proud parents of a lovely little girl. Contrary to all their friends' expectations, Phil is a doting and very competent father. Julia went back to work part time soon after Katia was born and Phil took on most of the daily chores of childcare. He and Katia are very close as a result and Phil claims never to have experienced a single regret about the manner of her conception:

She could not possibly feel more like my own child than she does already. Strangers who do not know the truth are always commenting how alike we are.

ADOPTION

Whatever the strains placed on a relationship by deciding to have an AID baby, it is at least the natural child of one partner. Adoption can require even more careful consideration before embarking on what is sometimes a painstakingly arduous, if ultimately rewarding, process. As in the case of AID, it is not something to be rushed into as a result of depression or panic about the discovery of one partner's infertility. It is best to take enough time to get over the initial feelings of grief or bitterness, so that the next moves may be decided objectively.

Finding out the facts about the availability of babies for adoption is the next step but it's not simply a question of choosing a new-born clone of oneself. Adoption agencies do the picking and choosing of prospective parents. Their priorities include such factors as age (the couple will be preferably under thirty-five), colour and 'suitability'. This last is strictly at the discretion of the agency but, sadly, may not always include the childless, as families who are already experienced in raising children may be considered a better environment for an older child with special problems. Couples who have been through divorce may also encounter a degree of opposition.

In spite of the 'market' pressure of considerable numbers of childless couples wanting to adopt, there are a large number of unwanted children, those of mixed races, those who have been in residential care for a long time, and the handicapped. Obviously these children are going to need a deep commitment and sensitive handling.

The fact that it is now possible for all adopted children to trace their natural mother or father once they have reached the age of eighteen has also led to a reduction in the number of babies being put forward for adoption. Living with the fear of having to face an unwanted offspring at some future time is not an inviting prospect for a panic-stricken pregnant teenager. All adoptions must also go through recognized agencies – private adoptions are illegal unless the proposed adopter is a relative of the child. Both these changes in the law have been made in the best interests of any child who is to be adopted. Unfortunately, they have also had the effect of making the adoption process even more difficult for the distressed and childless couple.

If you are lucky enough to fulfil the criteria for a 'suitable' couple, parenthood is still not instantaneous. There is a period of probation to go through before the law accepts the child as a legal member of the family. During this time the prospective parents must live with the possibility that the natural parents might reclaim their child at any moment.

Brian and Helen felt they had run an emotional marathon when, having survived all the searchingly intimate interviews and selection procedures as prospective adopters, an unexpected phone call informed them that they could collect a two-month-old baby boy from a hospital that night. They were told that the natural parents, although very distressed, had decided they were too young to cope with the financial and emotional responsibility of a child. They wanted it adopted. Here it was, at last.

There followed eight months of hard work and happiness as

the new baby filled their lives. Then there was a call from their adoption agency. The child's natural father wanted to meet Brian to 'explain why had given up his son'. Brian was strongly advised against this and refused, although reluctantly. There followed three months of unease, punctuated by the celebrating of baby Ben's first birthday. Then came the bombshell, the natural parents laid claim for the return of their child.

This was some kind of cruel and unusual punishment. They loved the baby, they wouldn't have been considered as adoptive parents if they had been incapable of loving him. Now they were going to lose Ben, not through illness or accident, but because the law was going to take him away. The build-up to the court case put intolerable pressures on Helen and Brian, the temptation to turn to tranquillizers for relief was very strong. By the day of the case, after weeks of legal flummery and form-filling, Helen was in a state of high anxiety while her husband was also drained of whatever emotional reserves were left.

There was no real contest between the rival claims, the hearing seemed brief to the point of banality. Ben was to be collected from their flat the same day and returned to the natural parents, who by now had apparently demonstrated their ability to offer the child a financially secure home.

Within a few months another child, a baby girl this time, was allocated to them but all did not go smoothly. Helen found herself unable to relax enough to start loving the little girl:

It was as though I had been Ben's natural mother and suddenly someone had come along, switched the babies over and told me to carry on caring for the new one. I could do everything that was necessary in the practical sense for Lucy but I couldn't give her what she needed most, a mother's love.

Luckily, Brian was both sensitive enough to the situation and strong enough to show affection for two until the time should come when Helen would recover from her grief and start to want Lucy to respond to her. One evening Brian arrived home to find Helen holding Lucy in her arms and weeping with emotion:

I knew it was all over then. Somehow we managed to survive for the remainder of the probationary period. The agency ran a discussion group for new parents and we soon discovered we were not the only ones who had experienced both the loss of a child and difficulties in relating to what can initially feel like a substitute. It made us both feel less alone and allowed us to admit to all the feelings we had been suppressing.

Lucy's adoption order proceedings were mercifully short. Brian and Helen took their first 'family' holiday together to celebrate both their baby and the relief of escape from the appalling emotional pressure of the previous months.

Not all adopting couples necessarily go through such a hard time. James, a thirty-two-year-old journalist, and his wife, Laura, also in her early thirties, began to act immediately they discovered the fact of Laura's untreatable infertility. For a while they considered the possibility of adopting a handicapped, slightly older child. Laura recalled:

I was mentally and physically prepared for this. I knew a little about it from having formed a fairly good relationship with the Down's syndrome child of a friend, but I don't think James was.

Coming from a large family of boisterous boys, James admits he had always seen himself as the romping-with-the-kids-with-a-football-on-Saturday-afternoons type:

I don't know if I am made of the sort of material it takes to stand up to the strain of a child with special needs. Looking back, I think it was lucky for me that I never had to find out.

While they were trying to make up their minds on the prospect of adopting a handicapped child, they received a phone call telling them a two-month-old baby girl would very soon be available, born to a Japanese student nurse who had refused an abortion (as her American boyfriend had wanted . . . he had now disappeared from the scene) but who instead, according to the adoption agency, had taken a deeply considered decision to have the child adopted.

There would be no courtroom battle but there was one request, that the baby should be named after her mother. James and Laura agreed that the baby should have both an English and a

Japanese name on her birth certificate. Rebecca Taeko is now three, perfectly integrated into her English family and eagerly waiting to start at nursery school. She is also just as excited by the thought that there is soon to be another addition to the family in the form of a second adopted child.

Laura still gets irritated when strangers comment on how lucky Rebecca Taeko is to have found a home like theirs:

It is we who feel privileged, we've had the luck. She's transformed our lives in a miraculously short time. We now have a future as a proper family.

ADAPTING TO CHILDLESSNESS

Not all stories of reluctant childlessness end so happily. There are always going to be infertile couples for whom neither science, adoption or AID is an answer. Not everyone is willing or able to submit themselves to the physical and emotional strains of investigation and treatment for infertility. Painful as it may be to admit, some people just feel that staying childless is preferable to nurturing someone else's child. Age will debar some from either option.

The outlook is not totally bleak, however. Many couples who have finally faced up to a future without children express surprise at the sudden relief they experienced just *when* any chance of a child was finally extinguished. There could be no more hope, but fellings of emptiness and anxiety also withered away. That was it . . . one aspect of human experience, the bearing and raising of children, had been denied but in its place was a challenge to cultivate and celebrate the rest of life.

Other big decisions like changing jobs, working abroad, creative challenges – things which may have been repeatedly deferred – come round again demanding attention. The couple's own relationship, which may have been under emotional siege for a long time because of infertility, can be put on a new basis with love and commitment being put back into each other rather than spilling all over the place in a heartbreaking search for an unattainable child. Forgetting the fertility factor can also rescue sex from the coldly mechanistic thing it may have become.

Coming to terms with not having children does not have to mean committing yourself to a life of isolation from young people. Close friendships with other couples can be very rewarding and can often lead to strong attachments to their children. Other routes include voluntary work and, of course, teaching. Quite often, naturally rebellious teenagers find it easier, as well as less emotionally complicated, to confide in family friends than their own parents.

The sight and sound of other people's 'happy families' can, however, still be a cruel reminder of one's own childlessnenss. For some it can seem too much to bear, but this is usually only a temporary phase. Time heals much and, as children grow to young adults and leave home, the gulf between those with children and those without starts to close.

There may also be more in common between those who choose consciously not to have children and those who want them but can't have them. There's one of those contemporary 'lifestyle' labels for couples who choose not to have children and, increasingly, infertile couples find solace in the more positive description 'childfree'. While still eaten up by a desire for an impossible conception, an honourable childfree existence seems remote if not inconceivable, but once reality has been confronted, talking to others who have a happy and fulfilling life without children can be very helpful. Self-help groups such as the National Association for the Childless are a very valuable source of advice and support.

From a purely objective point of view, life without children can be very attractive, and not just for material reasons. There should be much more freedom, money and time for self-expression, for career and creative fulfilment. But what about emotional fulfilment?

Divorce statistics for childless couples are substantially lower than for those with children. Why should this be? Depth of commitment to a partner could be greater or made so through weathering the disappointment of infertility together. However, for some women, many of the problems of the midlife, the feeling of frustration and sense of lost opportunities while bringing up children and the feelings of uselessness once children have been raised, for example, simply do not arise. Retirement need hold no horrors for them – in our society very few children remain close enough to their parents to be considered a comfort in old age.

Patrick and Gemma, both teachers in their late fifties, had to come to terms with Patrick's inability to father children thirty years previously. Gemma says that in spite of her desperate longings to be a parent herself, she had never wanted to adopt a child:

I wanted Patrick's child. If I couldn't have that I didn't want to have anyone else's. My work as a teacher has brought me satisfaction and almost as great a degree of fulfilment as I could have expected if I had been a mother myself. In fact I sometimes think I could not have put nearly so much into my teaching if I had had to cope with my own children when I got home in the evening.

When our friends' children began to grow up and move away, a subtle change seemed to take place in our relationship with them. Those who had tended to sometimes act rather patronisingly towards us for not knowing anything about child rearing suddenly seemed to be coming to us for advice on all sorts of topics. These were personal as well as practical, ranging from marital rows (and affairs) to how best to spend their increased leisure time.

Patrick agrees that friends changed from treating him like a teenager to consulting him like some elder statesman:

They thought I must have a lot of the answers to coping with late middle age. It startled me because I realized at that point that maybe they were right. The tragedy of my infertility had actually taught me skills in dealing with whatever else life might throw in my direction.

Acceptance of something which can't be cured and must be endured is not a negative act. If the pattern we (and perhaps our parents and partner also) expected is suddenly found not to fit, it is more than possible to create an equally valid alternative. The ability to make that transition successfully is the mark of growing emotional maturity.

Whatever patterns we have chosen in our twenties we tend to reweave in our thirties. The biological facts mean that the first shock waves of midlife crisis hit women before they hit men. No matter what is happening in the rest of our lives, the end of the ability to bear children causes a personal reappraisal. If we conclude that we are not where we want to be, there's not much time left to change things.

The end of the thirties therefore is a time of intensive stocktaking and introspection for a woman. Questions crowd in: 'My career is stuck, where do I go, what shall I do next? Another baby? A first baby? Am I able to have a baby? Back to work – at what level, do I have to start all over again? Am I happy with my husband? Divorce? Do I have to look for somebody else? Would anybody else want me?'

The most important question of all, the answer to which will have a big effect on our passage through midlife, is 'am I happy with myself? If not, what the hell am I going to do about it?'

Knowing that we are not alone in having to find answers to these questions, and that others have managed to steer their way successfully around the obstacles of the thirties into a happy midlife, helps us to accept the inevitability of this period of unsettlement. We have to go back to basics before we can build a secure foundation to tackle the great challenges that still lie ahead of us.

4

Midlife and beyond

We live in an ageist society. We fear the first grey hair and the spread of lines around our eyes because these are the outward signs of becoming non-persons – becoming old. Men who continue to take pride in their appearance are often described as 'distinguished'. Women who do the same are derided as 'mutton dressed as lamb' and ridiculed for refusing to grow old gracefully.

The notion that women are commodities, whose resale or trade-in value depends not so much on their personalities or talents but on their ability to attract men and produce children is deeply ingrained in our culture. Once this task is fulfilled, once all that birds-and-bees stuff about scented blooms and ripening pods is well and truly behind us, once we no longer serve any decorative or reproductive function, we may as well resign ourselves to becoming one of the stereotypes designated for us, the nagging wife or the malicious mother-in-law. Ask any actress – where are the great roles for women after, say, thirty-five? There's a prolonged period of 'resting' between playing Ophelia and Lady Bracknell.

With the average life-expectancy of women in developed countries now standing at seventy-five plus, more than a third of our allotted span is still to be looked forward to after the menopause. It seems absurd to consign such a large proportion of our lives to the scrapheap. There's a whiff of rebellion in the air. Older women are muscling their way back into the mainstream of popular culture. Just look at how, in the realm of soap opera, a powerful woman, the mother of seemingly endless children but still able to outslink any twenty-year-old upstart, is the dominant figure.

71

Now nobody's going to say that Alexis Carrington represents a triumph of feminist ideals but, although they may still manipulate men through sex, when they come out of the powder-room the soap queens get straight down to the million-dollar deals on their own terms. While what happens in the fantasy world of the soaps may have no bearing on real life, at least it reflects a broader cultural shift, a change in the way the role and utility of middle-aged women is perceived. Suffering in silence, being the shoulder to cry on, is right out. The middle-aged woman is at last wresting control of her own life.

For take control she must if she is going to be able to cope with those around who are still looking for support, while keeping her own identity intact and on the rails to a destination of her choosing. Her children are growing up, they might be in late teens or early twenties, but there will still be a strong backwash of emotional turbulence blowing through the family. She is likely to be the daughter of living parents who are getting frail and dependent. As the woman in the family, it is she who will be expected to shoulder the burden of 'caring'. She is the wife of a husband who expects support through his own set of midlife wobbles. She may be reaching a critical point in her own professional career. On top of this comes the menopause, the end of her ability to bear children, and her own middle-life angst. Who cares for the carer's own ambitions? Who cares for the carer's own needs? Unless we recognize them ourselves and act positively to sort them out, we end up not being able to help anyone.

To minimize the natural mix of anxiety and depression that looms as the menopause approaches, it is worth distinguishing the myths from the realities straightaway. There is no firm evidence that any psychological changes take place, other than as a result of each woman's individual reaction to the physical changes that occur – loss of periods, loss of fertility, hot flushes. Hot flushes are still not really understood but are thought to be a result of a number of factors combined with an instability in the hypothalamus, the portion of the brain which governs the body's hormonal cycle and the autonomic nervous system. Fifteen per cent of women experience no symptoms at all. It seems certain that emotional tension, if not wholly responsible for any special problems associated with the menopause, certainly exaggerates them. These can be numerous, ranging from insomnia and instability, to depression and loss of sex drive.

All these symptoms are closely connected with our perception of ourselves, our families and our lifestyles. Our ability to change our lives, or even to be conscious of a degree of control, is dependent upon both the patterns set for us (and that largely means by our own mothers) and by our own life-experience to date.

The middle-aged woman in the late 1980s has more problems as well as more opportunities than her mother had. She is under attack on several fronts. Look at the perils she may face at one remove, through the vulnerability of her own children to unemployment, drugs, sexually transmitted disease, compulsive behaviour patterns such as anorexia which would have been unheard of in her own ration-book childhood.

The outlook is not all black, however. There are also many possibilities for the mature woman to make an exciting future for herself. Her only limitation is likely to be her own low self-esteem, for freedom comes at the cost of having to assume personal responsibility; something which may come hard for a woman who has possibly spent the previous twenty years living through or relying upon other's experiences. As we have seen to a lesser extent in the case of the young mother at home, isolation and lack of contact with the outside world can lead quickly to loss of self-confidence, anxiety, depression and agoraphobia. How much more difficult it must be for the woman who has passed almost a third of her life struggling against such feelings to finally overcome them and break out.

The fear of this freedom underlies many of the psychological problems that lead to dependency upon tranquillizers or alcohol amongst older women today. Both anxiety and depression are easily translated into psychosomatic complaints. We are naturally reluctant to face the true origins of such illnesses as mental problems are stigmatized and shunned in a way that physical disease is not. It is difficult for doctors, once they have actual anatomical illnesss, to do anything but prescribe a course of tranquillizers. It is only recently that there has been any medical criticism of the over-prescribing of such drugs. Evidence of widespread real dependency and withdrawal problems has begun to alarm the GP at the front-line surgery level. 'Mother's little helper' has caused more misery among middle-aged women than the 'disease' it was prescribed to cure. Unfortunately a harassed GP cannot write a prescription for a new life-plan, which is what many such women are seeking.

Instead, sudden lack of direction as a family grows up, a blocked career or an empty marriage can cause overwhelming emotional pressure that leads, for some women towards escape through self-destruction. If this continues for any length of time, breaking out of an obsessive behaviour pattern becomes more and more difficult. A recent study shows that in all but two countries of the European Community two thirds of tranquillizer and anti-depressant drug users were women aged fifty-five and over.

Given this dispiriting weight of evidence anyone might be forgiven for expecting the worst when she hits forty. Anticipating problems we have not yet actually encountered may seem a bit daft but it's entirely understandable. It gives us a chance to stand outside the problem and assess our own individual prospects of emotional survival before our own frail craft hits the white water of the midlife rapids.

Some women may need expert help to be able to do this effectively but the majority are capable of coping alone as long as they understand what is happening to them. Feelings of confusion lead only to fear and a sense of powerlessness. Each one of us has to come to terms with the inevitability of the ageing process and handle it in our own individual way.

Just as in adolescence, we now have to be able to make a compromise between how things are and how we would ideally like them to be, and get on with the job instead of withdrawing when the emotional going gets tough. This is what maturity is really all about. It is the ability to make the imaginative leap into believing that we have the power to change what we do not like in ourselves or in our surroundings. Later life can be just as exciting and exhilarating as our youth if only we can approach it with the same degree of enthusiasm.

Sarah is a forty-three-year-old ex-model. As her fortieth birthday began to loom closer, she became increasingly depressed:

I had two failed marriages in my life, an undistinguished modelling career and no children. When I reviewed my life I felt that I hadn't achieved anything of note and, worst of all, the one thing that I had always relied on to grant me an easy passage through life – my looks – was about to desert to me for ever.

Although friends tried to reassure her about her attractiveness, Sarah grew more and more disturbed as she sought desperately to formulate some more fulfilling pattern in her life. All she was sure of was the way she had lived so far was not sufficient to sustain her through the second half:

I was aware that my youth had been swallowed up in superficiality. I thought about a facelift but that would only be like some kind of disguise. I was determined to find a new and more meaningful direction for my ambition. I had always had a close relationship with my sister's handicapped daughter. During this traumatic period I found myself spending more and more time with her. Gradually I realized that here was something that satisfied my longing to contribue to someone else's happiness. I had never really been needed before.

Since then Sarah has completed a teacher's training course and is now very happy working in a children's residential home. Sarah's particular problem – wanting to be needed, is an example of the middle-aged woman's search for self-justification but for many women problems arise directly from having so many emotional commitments that they feel they cannot afford the time to try and sort themselves out.

Forty-five-year-old Simone had spent the twenty-five years since she had left her native Jamaica catering to the needs of her extended family as well as working long and irregular hours as a midwife. Trapped midway between the generations, she now found herself caring both for her parents, her husband and ten-year-old son, as well as her twenty-two-year-old working daughter's two under-fives. She was totally exhausted, physically and emotionally, something which all those around her seemed not to notice.

When Simone went to her GP, she said nothing about this. What she described was a list of symptoms such as insomnia, migraine, nausea and irritability. She hastened to add that all this was 'merely menopausal' but she felt she could be helped by something she had read about, hormone replacement therapy.

Her doctor was more than willing to refer her to the menopause clinic at her local hospital, but was also aware of her family circumstances and the pressure that she was under. Sensitive to her pride, he encouraged her to confide in him. To her own surprise Simone found herself opening up, likening her daily existence to being trapped on a treadmill, admitting that all her once-cherished hopes and ambitions were now just trampled on by her family:

I went home feeling that some significant turning-point in my life had been reached that afternoon. I did attend the hospital for HRT, but I also enrolled for a course in counselling that was to last for two years and which totally altered my perspective on my life.

Simone now runs a counselling course for nurses and others in the 'caring' professions such as social workers and teachers. She finds it immensely satisfying and stimulating and thinks that she is still learning about how to deal with the excessive demands of those around her. Obviously the transformation from depressed menial into self-assertive manager was not instantaneous. It involved many heroic failures and ensuing family rows. But eventually Simone managed to get her message across (and even to start believing herself) that not only did she possess the power to change her life, but that she had an inalienable right to an intellectual and emotional life outside the sphere of her dependents:

Women have to be able to set limits upon their responsibilites in order not to be overwhelmed by them. The first thing I did was to allocate domestic tasks to each of my family and make it clear that from now on there were going to be times when I would be 'unavailable' to them because I now had something to do of my own. Even saying the words gave me a thrill of achievement. I am slowly learning the art of self-assertion. It is fascinating to see what a difference it has made both to my own life and to the lives of the women I now work with.

Simone's case history is very typical – a woman suffering from a degree of physiological menopausal problems, exacerbated by the emotional strains of her everyday life. Her doctor very sensibly helped her to deal with them himself by first untangling them and then confronting each one in turn.

The search for self-identity

For a woman with family responsibilities stretching, perhaps, from caring for her parents to handling the turmoils of adolescent children, there's not much time left to worry about her own identity. It has long been acceptable for older adolescents to disappear to some far-off continent in order to 'find' themselves. This kind of self-obsession is perfectly all right for a teenager, but at forty it is seen as deranged or, at the very least, undignified.

How are we ever to define ourselves anyway? By middle age a large part of our life will have been spent trying to act out a series of changing roles, like some B-movie actress always learning a new script doled out by central casting – sex object, wife, sex object, mother, non-sex object, working mother, daughter, woman alone and so on. When we have to go back to being ourselves the scripts are running dry. Unfortunately, we cannot remember who we were in the first place, or we never had sufficient time to work it out before we assumed the part. The menopause represents the greatest *entr'acte* of all and is therefore often a time of crisis, but also a time of compromise, a time for emotional reserves to be renewed.

In the course of a marriage a woman has to assume several different roles. Before the menopause she is wife and mother, holding the centre stage of family life but gradually, as the children grow up and depart, her role shrinks to a walk-on part. However, there is no need for enforced emotional redundancy as long as she can stay flexible and adapt herself to the changed internal politics of the family.

She will have lost power but if she can accept this with equanimity, offering her children wisdom and experience, the transition will work. Changing attitudes towards sex, work, independence and the role of women need not cause a gulf between young and old if they can be discussed with equal respect on both sides. A mother has to accept her young adult children pushing out the boundaries of their independence but she is still entitled to provide a safety-net of advice even if it is spurned. As soon as babies appear on the horizon, she will be very much in demand, sometimes too much, but grand-motherhood can be a uniquely fulfilling time in a woman's life.

At the age of eighteen Jacqui was a rebellious and troublesome teenager. She had been on drugs charges although she had miraculously managed to avoid conviction each time. Her parents Frank and Louise were both in their early forties and strict churchgoers. They were appalled by her behaviour and internal family communications had all but broken down. Finally, after deserting college in her first term and running off with a fellow student, her father, in his own words, 'Washed my hands of the whole affair. I've done the best I can and it's still no good. I give up on her.'

Louise pleaded with her husband not to be so harsh, but he remained adamant in his refusal to speak to Jacqui even when she became pregnant.

In the meantime, Louise was quietly going through a crisis of her own. Jacqui's departure could not have come at a worse time for her. Just as she was realizing she would never be able to bear a longed-for second child, not only was her first-born gone but, due to Frank's harshness, looked like being lost for ever.

A frantic midnight phone call while Frank was away led to Louise and her daughter being reunited. Jacqui saw for the first time how vulnerable her mother was as Louise's own fears about the future of her marriage, and her regret of the lack of an independent career came tumbling out:

Talking to Jacqui, I suddenly realized just how adult she had become. She seemed a lot more sorted out than I was myself at that age, and I actually found myself asking her advice.

Happily this process worked both ways, Frank was reluctantly

78

persuaded to accept Jacqui back in the house. Mother and daughter worked out a rota of daily babycare and both started attending a local college, Jacqui to read Law and Louise Accountancy. Louise had recognized far more than Frank that their child was grown up and demanded a different response from them as parents. She gained as much from the new kind of interaction with her daughter as she was able to put back. Gradually even Frank had to accept his 'new' daughter and grandchild and they are now full reconciled.

Parent–child relationships

Just at the time we may be looking round for reassurance, that last resort, that place we have turned to before when the going got too tough, is no longer there. Our parents may become increasingly frail and emotionally dependent on us. They may already be dead. The death of one or both of our parents finally forces us to the front of the queue. There can be no pretence of youth, no compromise with mortality.

It is important not to let this growing realization of our parents' needs push us into being over-supportive too soon since this can chip away at their independence and injure their pride. If they are still capable of managing by themselves, frequent visits and phone calls are often enough to reassure everyone concerned. It needs a great deal of tolerance and understanding to take either your own or your husband's parents into the home just at the moment of adult release achieved when the children have finally grown up and gone.

For the single woman who is an only child, this kind of self-sacrifice can of course spell the end of any independent relationship, and indeed, a career.

Paula was a junior civil servant on a good salary. Determination and a practical and hardworking approach towards life had led her slowly up the promotional ladder. The early retirement of her immediate boss looked like a chance to grab the highest rung. However, she was the only child of elderly parents. She was well aware that one or other of them might die at any time, leaving her to care for the other one. She tried to bury such thoughts as she might shove a discomforting memo to the back of the in-tray. Unfortunately for Paula, her father's death coincided with her important job opportunity. Her mother seemed to take for granted not only that she would come and live with her daughter, but also that Paula would leave work and come and look after her full time.

The strain was terrible. The inner conflict of guilt, duty and ambition threatened to overwhelm Paula in a full-blown midlife crisis. Her work began to suffer as insomnia, anxiety and indecision sapped her concentration. Tranquillizers and sleeping pills gave a kind of support but Paula was wary that the 'hangovers' they produced were as harmful to her work performance as the emotional roots of her trouble themselves. She knew that if she gave in to her mother not only would this one career-chance slip away but she would become embittered and frustrated. Yet the alternative of putting her mother into a home was unbearable. Being so close to the problem she was unable to stand back far enough to decide objectively what to do. There seemed no way out, the emotional turmoil was insupportable.

Confiding in a loyal and close friend who was able to see the situation from outside, as well as having the mother and daughter's best interests at heart, proved to be Paula's salvation. The friend was able to point out that Paula's mother was being exceptionally selfish and expecting far too much from her daughter at the expense of the future happiness of them both. She deserved to be cared for but not at the cost of Paula's career.

Paula realized the wisdom of this at once:

It was really what I had been feeling all the time but was reluctant to admit because of my guilt about her. Even my thoughts seemed to be censored by my conscience while I was under such emotional pressure. Hearing it from someone else allowed me to acknowledge my own feelings.

She at last felt able to discuss the problem with her mother and to try and work with her towards a mutually acceptable solution. There is often no right decision in a case like this and the issues involved are bound to remain sensitive for some time. Paula eventually decided that her mother should come to live with her but that she would continue with her career and the self-contained life that had become precious to her. She was in the fortunate position of being able to hire a housekeeper once she had got her promotion.

For every woman in Paula's financial position there are a thousand who cannot afford domestic or nursing help. The extent of this problem, and even the very existence of these self-sacrificing women, has only recently been acknowledged in the Government's agreement to pay them an invalid care allowance.

Paula was also wise enough to see that her mother was in need of social stimulus to avoid becoming emotionally overdependent upon her:

I encouraged her to start new friendships through interests outside the home. I realized that both she and my father had seen less and less of their friends once my father became ill, and I felt she had become rather isolated.

Her mother was at first suspicious of what she refered to as her daughter's 'bossiness' but she gradually settled down to the idea of having a separate existence once more and even started to enjoy herself with her new circle of friends and neighbours.

The change that Paula saw in her mother was a direct result of her own emotional development. Simply being middle-aged need not be a cause for terminal gloom on its own – if we can witness the positive effects of our personal growth on the generations on either side of us.

Worlds to conquer

On a much wider level, 'mature' women have an enormous contribution to make to the wisdom of world politics. It is no accident that there have been many older women so committed to the cause of peace that they are willing to endure the scorn of the Press and public opinion, as well as physical discomfort in order to make their point at Greenham Common and elsewhere.

The crusading spirit of a middle-aged, experienced woman can be a formidable thing, not as easily dismissed as that of an excitable adolescent, and it deserves to be heeded.

Mature adult women who change the pattern of their lives do so with an awareness of the result of their personal change upon others. Growth in middle age is different from the adolescent voyage of self-discovery; it has the added dimension of concern for the human condition.

Now, really for the first time in our culture, we are beginning to see the focus of public attention falling on the previously much-neglected middle-aged woman. More and more radio and stage plays, films, novels and documentaries are being made both by and about women in their forties. This is in itself a good sign since the more women realize their full potential, the greater will be their influence in altering the patronizing attitude of society towards them.

Partnership and middle life

A working microcosm of just such a male – female coalition can be seen in the family. Women are not the only ones to face the personal crisis of middle age. It is possible to help both ourselves and our partners through this traumatic time, into a deepened and enriched relationship, if we can be sensitive enough to what the other person may be experiencing.

In theory, men and women reaching middle age simultaneously should be able to have more time for each other. In practice, however, all too often the departure of children is like being left stranded on a desert island with a stranger whose language you cannot understand. It suddenly highlights the fact that two lives have been drifting in different directions for so long that the gap has become almost impossible to close. As with strangers, we have to start all over again if we still have the motivation to make it work. Sometimes there is nothing left worth salvaging. Relationships are delicate and need regular care and attention to keep them in good working order. Prolonged neglect or lack of communication can do irreparable damage.

The death of a marriage through deliberate neglect is sad, the loss of a partner through absent-minded insensitivity is a tragedy.

At its best middle age provides an opportunity for a second chance in a partnership to look at each other with new clarity and to make or maintain stronger links. Unless we do this it is impossible to offer each other the mutual support and encouragement necessary for further individual development.

Everyone needs an ego-boost now and then and never more so than when increasing numbers of lines and grey hairs are detected in the mirror each morning. Low self-worth, depression, anxiety and lack of self-confidence can all be combatted by the encouragement and reassurance of a loving partner. Demonstrative evidence of an enduring and reliable affection can renew flagging belief in ourselves and our potential, despite fading looks or loss of physical stamina. It engenders hope and a realization that the loss of youth is not necessarily the loss of purpose or the loss of love.

Social and intellectual stimulus are especially important at this time. Getting involved in new activities and remaining open to new ideas are the keys to the continuation of an active and fulfilling existence. Where both partners are busy with their own plans and schemes, the interchange of thoughts and opinions becomes mutually rewarding and exciting. It is most often when one partner is fulfilled and the other frustrated that resentment and envy begin to creep in and put their mutual happiness in jeopardy.

Happiness in love and work are interdependent and both are equally important in getting the emotional balance right. A man approaching retirement will need his wife's help in coming to terms with what he may feel as a loss of status in society, while she may require reassurance from him of her competence to return to the world of work. In this way both partners can become more fully rounded as they get the chance to develop qualities and skills previously associated with the opposite sex. The man may, for the first time, feel free to display emotion while the woman may discover ambition and drive she had not realized she possessed. This in itself will tend to lead to a deeper understanding and affection between them.

Paul, a structural engineer of fifty-three, had been devoted to his job for twenty-five years and was dreading his approaching retirement. Never having had many interests or hobbies outside work he found it impossible to envisage a future without the regimen of nine to five. His forty-five-year-old wife, May, was worried about both their futures since now that their two children were away at college she was beginning to sense a certain lack of direction in her own life:

I had always regretted not having a career of my own although I enjoyed the years I had spent at home. It had never really occurred to me that it was still possible to pick up new skills at my age until I saw an advertisement for a data processing course. I had kept up my shorthand and typing and was secretly delighted to discover how easily I acquired new techniques, including computer programming.

May could not understand her husband's disapproving and bitter attitude. Paul began to criticize her constantly, often generating rows between them in the process. At first May ignored him but it had soon escalated to a point where Paul was indulging in uncharacteristic bouts of heavy drinking and suffering from fits of depression. May finally managed to persuade him to talk it over:

It was the first time I ever found him crying. He said he saw no future ahead of him and that my excitement and energy had only emphasized his own inertia and unhappiness.

Once May understood the cause of his destructive behaviour, she determined to save both Paul's self-respect and their marriage. She suggested he apply for a part-time vacancy as a clerical officer in the projects department of their local housing association. Initially hostile towards the idea, Paul finally agreed to at least attend for interview. A year later, having discovered Paul's training and talents, the director was offering him more and more responsibility, as he became increasingly involved with the human side of working with the homeless, May was amazed at the change in their relationship:

What strikes me most is how excited we both are. Now we rush home in the evening eager to exchange news. Paul is far more caring and sympathetic towards me than he used to be and is genuinely interested in my success. Our marriage now seems to have more going for it than it did twenty years ago when our lives were locked into the traditional breadwinner/wife-at-home roles.

Some sort of proof that we are still sexually attractive is vital at a time when we may feel that our femininity as well as our fertility is starting to wane. For some middle-aged women (and men too) this leads to our seeking out this proof in the form of an extramarital affair. This may provide short-term physical and emotional relief but it remains a way of evading the real issue – that any number of new partners will not restore our lost youth to us. In order to come to terms with ageing it is essential to see that it need not be such a negative process and that both intellectual and sexual stimulus can still elicit response in both partners. The loss of a woman's periods is not a sign that she should give up sexual intercourse and for many women the release from the fear of pregnancy can intensify enjoyment.

Sexual experimentation is a way of breaking out of a pattern of lovemaking which may have become boring or predicatable. With the children grown up and some of the pressures and responsibilities of parenthood relieved, the couple may be able to recapture a more carefree and relaxed approach to their sex life as the conflict between the roles of parent and lover is finally removed.

Each partner can help to improve the other's self-image, not just through sex itself but also through the emotional reassurance of tenderness, respect and imaginative seduction techniques. Maturity also provides us with the freedom to express our sexual desires with less embarrassment than in our youth, whilst shared experiences enables us to see the other person as a multilayered individual rather than as a single-faceted sex object.

Confirmation of our still powerful sexual identity helps to dismiss emotional insecurity and should allow us to face the future with renewed confidence.

The future is no longer the vast uncharted sea of potential that we dreamt of in our youth. We are by now aware of certain personal failings and physical limitations but, having survived the emotional turbulence of earlier years, at least the far shore is in sight. Skilful navigation is still required if we are to reach it safely with a sense of achievement at the end of our lives, rather than with unhappy feelings of frustration or disappointment.

Fifty-five plus

The span of a woman's life-expectancy, in the affluent northern hemisphere at least, is up to a decade longer than that of her male partner. It is therefore simple prudence to try and gain a certain amount of self-reliance and happiness in our own company before the statistical majority of us have to face that final enforced separation.

Some women can't face it and use their children as a means of providing some sort of stimulation. No woman wants to intrude on the lives of her grown-up children unnecessarily. Those women who do take interference too far tend to do it out of a sense of terror of uselessness, a desperation that they will be left in the solitary confinement of their own homes without any real role. We are all familiar with the language of their hurt pride: 'I don't want to be a burden on anyone,' or 'Don't worry about me, I am perfectly capable of looking after myself.' We also know how hollow these protestations can be.

We might remain physically competent as we get older, but whether we are emotionally equipped to deal with loneliness in old age is quite a different matter. The resources for independent survival are there, even though they may be buried very deep. It is all a question of learning to tap them. Living alone does not need to be a desolate experience, it can be immensely satisfying to realize (just as in the case of divorce) that, even after years of believing one's existence inextricably linked to another's, independence is not only possible but positively enjoyable. First we have to learn to love ourselves: something which is often so much harder to achieve than loving someone else. If the main object of our love, our partner, is no longer there, of course there is going to be a gaping hole in our lives for a while. Being left suddenly alone means having to deploy the same emotional skills that would have helped us all the way through. It is useful if we have managed to pick them up before but it is still possible to start learning them now.

Ironically, the death of a husband frees a woman for her ultimate role. If her own parents are already dead she is no longer the daughter, with her children grown-up and gone away she is no longer needed as a full-time mother; now the curtain descends on her role as wife. All that remains is for her to play the last and most demanding part of all in the final act – herself.

By the time she reaches this stage a woman will have witnessed much exchanging of roles around her as well – her parents will have become like children and her children may be parents themselves. Her priorities will also have altered. The ambitious career woman, whether or not she has reached her goal or been left disappointed, may by now be disillusioned. A job is only, in the last analysis, a job.

So what is left once we have ceased to blame our parents, our children or our spouse for our personal problems? The frightening knowledge we all have to face sooner or later is that ultimately we are all alone, that there is going to be a time when no one can help us or reach out to us. Reassurance rings hollow then, for we know we are responsible for, and must rely upon ourselves. We also realize once and for all that it is unrealistic to expect others to understand us but this no longer matters for the luxury of this state is that we become our own first priority.

Putting yourself first does not mean going on a spree of self-indulgence. It can mean feeling free for the first time to do what you want and say what you think without fear of others' disapproval; a one-off opportunity to be wholly yourself. Naturally, there will also be times when you desperately miss the one you have lost, and you will suffer from acute loneliness, as opposed to just being alone. Missing someone because you loved them is a natural and deserving tribute to their memory, missing them because you cannot bear to be alone can be considered insulting to that same memory. For far too many widows there is a larger element of the second mixed in with the first, mainly because our society has dictated to us that to lose one's husband is to lose our identity. It need not be so if we can prepare ourselves beforehand for life after bereavement.

Nobody needs to be morbidly anticipating the death of a husband to get enjoyment from cultivating interests and friendships outside the home. Mental stimulation is an essential aid to fighting off loneliness or depression at any stage of life – the more exposed we are to a wide range of opinions, the more chance we stand of maintaining a well-balanced viewpoint ourselves. Total emotional and intellectual investment in any one individual is both unfair and unrealistic. 'I couldn't go on living without you' is a good line but as a statement of fact it just isn't true. We can and do have to survive the deaths of those we love however unacceptable the thought may be. Suicide or self-immolation is not a reflection of a singular devotion but an indication of an internal unhappiness.

FACING UP TO WIDOWHOOD

It is not solitude alone that makes widowhood hard to bear. It's also having to scale the mountains of financial and other problems that sometimes seem to have grown into soaring peaks overnight. It is far better to grapple with these beforehand, since the additional emotional anxiety of bereavement tends to exaggerate our everyday worries. There is help at hand – friends, family, or such organizations as CRUSE whose specially trained counsellors can provide practical as well as emotional support.

Sympathy is not always what we need at times of emotional distress. Talking to someone who has been through and obviously survived a similar experience as ourselves is often far more helpful and reassuring, which is why self-help groups have been so successful in so many areas of both physical and emotional illness.

The National Association of Widows, for example, is a rapidly growing self-help programme run by widows for widows which holds regular meetings and can be of particular assistance with the practical problems of widowhood as well as being good as a source of communal support.

Sixty-one-year-old Lena lost her husband Henry when he fell down the stairs of their new home two months before he was due to retire from his demanding job as an executive of an international company. For years they had both been looking forward to the time when they would be able to relax enough to have some time to themselves, and Lena felt angry and cheated 'almost as though Henry's death had been deliberate'.

With two sons in their twenties both away at college, she knew she was going to have to sort her life out for herself if she was going to be able to avoid depression and loneliness:

It was an emotional body-blow. I couldn't seem to understand my own reaction. Above everything else, I felt guilty and angry over the accident. I traced the event back in my mind a thousand times. I blamed myself for not being there when it happened, for the row we had that morning, even moving house in the first place.

I was unhappy for a long time. I wanted to talk about Henry endlessly but no one wanted to listen because they felt it was 'bad' for me. But it wasn't at all – it was vital.

Lena made contact with CRUSE after hearing about them on a radio phone-in, and arranged to talk to a bereavement counsellor. 'It all came flooding out in a rush, she recalled, 'all those pent-up feelings of misery, pain and resentment. The relief was incredible.'

Lena is now slowly picking up the pieces of the post-retirement life that she and her husband Henry had planned. She fits in as much social activity as she can, as well as organizing work projects for herself. One of the first things she did was to sit down and write about her husband's death and how she felt about it. She discovered that this was not only a way of releasing tension but that she also had a talent that she enjoyed. Since then, with the help of a bank loan, she has bought herself a word processor and written several successful features for women's magazines:

I now feel able to accept the fact of Henry's death. I've been through the loneliness and have learnt how to fight it and win. It sounds silly at my age but I am into a new and exciting phase of my life.

Once Lena had allowed herself the necessary mourning of loss, she felt able to 'let go' of her husband without losing her memories of him. She had also helped this healing process along by working at it.

Getting over grief needs work and effort. There are no easy options. Retirement and old age are not an excuse for surrendering to depression and self-pity. As long as there are challenges before us (which is as long as we are alive) we have to keep confronting them if we are to continue the process of self-discovery. There is no miracle prescription, no Elixir of Life to carry us through old age on a wave of optimism. It is within our power to change our lives if we want to—to make them more positive, more exciting and ultimately far more rewarding than sitting back and allowing ourselves to be overtaken by nebulous fears and regrets for what might have been.

5

Mother – daughter – mother

Much has been written in fiction and in the literature of human relationships about the complex dynamic that exists between mother and daughter. Yet it still emerges regularly in my caseload as one of the major causes of emotional confusion and misery among women of all ages. Why this should be and whether we are capable of working out our own ambivalent attitudes towards the most loving and yet most fraught of emotional ties are obviously questions we might benefit from considering for, sooner or later, we must be able to break that maternal bond in order to achieve a mature and separate identity of our own – but the story does not end there.

If we manage to make the break successfully, separation need not mean the end of love. The genuinely mature woman will be able to reforge that link from her own newly found strengths as an individual and also, perhaps, from the empathy that flows from having become a mother herself. Discovering a separate identity must involve rebellion. We have to reject the internal dictator (the mother-image) in order to set up our own republic. Once the revolution has been made, the power politics have changed. 'Mother' is no longer the indestructible enemy whose very presence can be seen as a threat to overwhelm us; she is capable of being an ally whose emotional support is now going to be a two-way affair, taken as well as given.

Unfortunately, for far too many of us the process of rebellion does not end in such a state of harmonious peace. If our emotional troops temporarily lack the strength to tear down the dictatorship, they are forced to retreat into hiding in our subconscious from where they make the occasional unsuccessful foray. Prolonged failure to assert independence leads to loss of morale, smouldering but subdued hostility and minor petty skirmishes. Until that internal dictator is finally deposed she will continue to stand between us and the attainment of a fulfilled and mature adulthood.

As we have seen, if this first relationship is not a satisfactory and happy one it is likely to have far-reaching effects upon all future relationships including those with our own daughters. In this way, unsolved problems can be transmitted across the generations.

Let's look back to those early days to see what can sometimes happen to cause a later conflict between the expression of self-identity and the role of 'daughter'. Since any infant's first relationship is usually with a female, a boy child will quickly come to experience himself as being 'separate' and different from her. A girl, however, will naturally see herself as being like her mother. Self-identification will lead towards rather than away from her. Later this can cause confusion over personal boundaries on both sides. Neither mother nor daughter can be clear or confident about where she ends and the 'other' begins. This is the source of many later dependency problems in partnerships where the man is perceived by the woman as having taken over the role she has not managed to work through with her mother. In this way she is held kidnapped in an emotional timewarp long after she may have become a mother herself. Her unsatisfied yearning for a love which she feels is undeserved then gets in the way to prevent her from fulfilling the emotional needs of her own daughters.

According to psychologists, full-blown attempts to separate from our mothers come at several stages of our lives: during childhood and adolescence and later when we leave home and start families of our own. An individual's success in achieving separate identity is not necessarily visible to the outside world and, in some cases, can be positively misleading. Often the most outgoing and free-spirited of women is in fact overcompensating for the little girl who still sobs inside her. Interpreting her own unfulfilled needs as a threat, she resolves to bury them in her subconscious and 'forget' them, but they refuse to go away and return to haunt her when she feels vulnerable or insecure. It is unfortunate that we can no more force ourselves to grow up than we can make ourselves less shy and more self-confident. If this were possible my postbag as an agony aunt could be instantly halved.

Natalie appears confident and self-assured; she seems ideally suited for her job as a PR consultant. Nothing, it seems, could ever betray the confused and sad little girl who still lives inside her. All her relationships with men have repeated the same disastrous pattern, beginning with an initial frostiness which gradually thaws into passionate intimacy, then there comes the sudden finality of a lightning emotional withdrawal and the relationship ends. Trying to come to terms with her own misery and confusion led her to start talking to her mother:

Her attitude to me was always ambivalent. I am sure she tried to show her love for me but I felt it to be self-conscious. She seemed like a stranger. Sometimes I think I even frightened her. Everyone else said I was a very grown-up little girl and I clung on to that and cultivated it – I haven't ever stopped doing that but it's always been a pretence. I never feel real.

Natalie had always had a longing for a close relationship with a man but had an equally strong simultaneous fear of rejection. Happy times were of short duration:

I then prime myself to self-destruct. The most trivial of excuses serves as evidence of unavailability, lack of love for me. Persistent recriminations lead to the rapid deterioration and ultimate annihilation of even my strongest relationships. I can neither understand or prevent it.

Understanding and coming to terms with these patterns of the past can help alter such compulsive and self-negating patterns in the present. For example, once Natalie began to trace her current problems back to their roots in her primary relationship with her mother, she realized that it was within her power to change.

Certainty of our mothers' unfailing love during infancy forms the foundation of our future self-confidence. As we grow older this secure base is necessary for the occasional retreat from the often frightening process of entering adulthood. Without it the affection of potential partners for us becomes much harder to handle – because of a sense of rejection in childhood, we just don't believe that we 'deserve' love, and we are immediately suspicious of anyone prepared to show it to us. If we can allow ourselves to let go for long enough to establish intimacy, we may believe for a short time that we have finally found someone to supply us with the nurturing we so desperately need. However, the expectation of renewed disappointment remains with us and, as in Natalie's case, requires very little justification to prove its point and condemn us once more to feelings of isolation, low self-worth and inadequacy.

What are these needs and why should they cause so much misunderstanding between ourselves and our mothers? Many women report a confusing ambivalence in their relationships with their mothers. They feel resentment and fear of her overwhelming control and yet simultaneously require more of her love and attention. They sense that their needs are not being met because her own dependency has never been worked through properly. She may even look to her own daughter to help her.

This can lead to a very complex and confusing exchange of messages. Her daughter pleads for love and security, the mother's response is that she needs it too but has learnt not to expect it. She instructs her to be a carer and a giver towards others and then concludes with a cry for help of her own.

Lesley had always been very close to her mother especially since her parents had divorced when she was sixteen. Her mother had relied on her for emotional support ever since and Lesley had been happy to provide it even after she had left home. However, at the age of twenty-eight, with a job, husband and children of her own laying claims on her, Lesley began to grow increasingly resentful of her mother's constant demands – but she felt guilty if she failed to respond to them. She was conscious that she wanted them both to become more independent of each other, but was also worried about inflicting unnecessary pain in the process. She decided finally that she had no option but to discuss it with her mother as tactfully as she could. It emerged that Lesley's mother had very mixed feelings, both about Lesley's emotional independence and her own. It is natural for mothers to identify with their daughters, and this often leads to confusion over who's actually caring for whom as the daughter reaches adulthood.

Mothers simultaneously want their daughters to be independent of them yet fear their own redundancy—so there is a constant emotional pull and push going on. Lesley's mother felt that it was Lesley who still needed her rather than the other way around. Sitting down and talking about it helped them both. The fact that they had always been close was very important to both of them. Neither wanted to lose that intimacy, so each was prepared to work at it. Lesley's mother had to have another go at growing up and Lesley was able to help her to do this gradually by encouraging her to widen her circle of friends. The relationship became less stifling and more satisfying—her mother's own independence freed Lesley to do some growing for herself and the push-pull dynamic was finally broken.

If an unhappy childhood relationship reaches out into adult life, the chances of reconciliation are not necessarily slim. Reparation for lost years of early love is always possible and, once the redress is complete, the texture of all our other relationships can be improved.

6

Unfinished business

Mothers and daughters are not the only ones who may have 'unfinished business' to sort out before they can complete their journey to maturity. Old loves, old hurts, past pleasures, past pain, anything which hasn't been worked through to an internally satisfying emotional conclusion can return quite literally to haunt us. Of course there is plenty going on in times present to remind us of times past but, more often than not, any fossilized emotions which are recalled from the subconscious and conscious Filofax of feelings we all drag around with us, are going to be unhappy ones. They are those that we have tried to suppress in the first place because we felt we were unable to deal with them at the time.

Summoning up spirits can be dangerous at the best of times. Exorcism is an exhausting but essential process if we are going to learn to face the future without the fear of a pack of spectral hurts and jealousies pursuing us from the past. These ghosts of unfinished business can disguise themselves in myriad forms. It may involve parents, brothers, sisters, authority, lovers or friends but, whatever the original cause, it can manifest itself in the shape of anxiety, depression, eating disorders or dependency on drugs or alcohol.

We have already seen how the experience of anorexia or abortion may leave a woman with a host of unworked-through feelings. She may claim to have got over these traumas but apparent emotional recovery can be deceptive. The 'cured' anorexic may turn to the compulsion of alcoholism. The woman who has chosen not to have a child may still suffer from intense secret guilt for years, even after the menopause. These feelings certainly won't go away on their own, and are even less likely to depart in peace while we continue to nurture them in silence. Facing up to their existence is the first and most difficult step on the road back to emotional health. Finding the right sort of help is the second.

Facing up to unfinished business

Women have it tough anyway. Even though we might be regarded as the emotional linchpin of family life with all its criss-crossing trails of relationships, as individuals we have a sense of political and social powerlessness. Already restricted by the limited role permitted us by society, we strengthen the bonds that bind us by the very lack of self-esteem this induces and just compound our dilemma. That's the condition of women; it won't change overnight and it does make us that much more vulnerable and more prone to drag round emotional loose ends than men might be.

If the emotional baggage of the past is not dealt with it can become a dragging burden. Old hurts which should have been consigned to the attic long ago can litter the centre-stage of our lives waiting to trip us up. If we should fall, it can be disastrous. Old feelings of resentment and frustration, unfulfilled longings, unresolved guilt can show up as physical symptoms or as compulsive behaviour patterns. Our inner fears can be transmuted into a phobia of some external object or situation, while our distress can be translated into psychosomatic symptoms whose origins can seem utterly baffling. Much pain and confusion ensues from both these states. This suffering is subconsciously self-inflicted – the victim has effectively separated herself from her bad feelings by projecting them either on to an illness or a fear of some specific 'outside' object or incident. However, she remains a victim at the mercy of the invader. She cannot visualize herself having any power to control what is going on around her. In this way she delegates responsibility to her doctor, parents or family. She is so frightened of what she interprets as the 'bad' part of her self and she passes the emotional buck and evades the blame. The body is both subject and master to the mind.

GETTING TO THE ROOT OF THE PROBLEM

Helping a woman to overcome a phobia or to dismiss a psycho-somatic symptom involves providing the reassurance of which she has so little reserve. Once she can incorporate the rejected feelings she will gradually be able to come to terms with herself. Until then she will continue to be a prisoner of her own bodily reactions.

Physical symptoms or phobic states represent only a temporary escape. For a time they can be a way of accepting the unacceptable but only until they begin to reproduce themselves. Fear of the unknown illness or phobia itself compounds anxiety and such complex layers are built one upon another that it becomes very difficult to dig deep enough to disentangle the sufferer.

Self-exploration through therapy is the most effective and long-lasting way of dealing with unfinished business. It can serve to distance us from the root of our troubles, thereby dividing us even further from ourselves. The passage to maturity requires the rites of confrontation, acceptance and absorption of that part of ourselves we have been running away from. The therapist can assist us in this by giving us back a true reflection of ourselves and by reassuring us that we are not about to be overwhelmed by our own 'bad' feelings. Getting back to basics may take some time. We may also have to triumph over some very powerful taboos.

Martina is a thirty-six-year-old social worker. The only child of an ill-matched couple who stayed together for her sake, she remembers a childhood full of longing for a sibling to relieve her loneliness and to share the weight of guilt for her parents' unhappiness. She had always felt closer to her father, who appeared very quiet, competent and self-contained, than to her mother who, in Martina's words, 'was frequently hysterical or neurotic and smoked and drank too much'. Martina escaped to university and subsequent marriage to a man markedly similar in personality to her much-loved father. At first she was very happy. She adored her husband, Robert, and thought him infinitely superior in intellect to herself. Gradually, however, she became aware that there was something missing in their relationship. Always absorbed in his work or a new novel, Robert often appeared unaware of her presence and seemed to feel no urge to share or communicate his feelings or experiences with her. During the course of eight years of marriage this led to several crises. Firstly, Martina's desperate search for emotional response led her into an extramarital affair. Robert feigned ignorance but withdrew his sexual favours, leaving her depressed and frustrated. Next she attempted to provoke a reaction by falling pregnant. Coldly hostile at first, Robert eventually 'came round' to the idea of fatherhood. For a time Martina felt less unhappy but, as their son grew up, the old feelings of desolate discontent began to return and eventually Martina sought relief in psychotherapy. What prompted her was the shocking realization that she had recreated exactly the memory she most hated and feared – that of her parents' empty marriage.

Unwittingly she had assumed her mother's role and was becoming increasingly reliant on alcohol and cigarettes to boost her rapidly diminishing ego. In the midst of Martina's emotional confusion one solid fact remained. She knew she still loved Robert and her determination to sort it all out grew from that fact.

As Martina recounted her early experiences to her therapist she began to unlock the doors on the memories she had hidden away:

I remember how I wanted to look after my father so that he would love me more than mother. I even dreamt that my mother was dead and Dad and I could live alone together for ever. I had never admitted these thoughts before to anyone. I felt a sense of overwhelming relief. My therapist had managed to reassure me that nothing awful was going to happen either to my mother or myself by allowing these thoughts to come to the surface. For the first time I began to feel sympathetic towards my mother and we were able to start communicating. It also gave me the confidence to persuade Robert to come to a Marriage Guidance counsellor with me.

The deepest layer of Martina's defences had finally been uncovered and the core of her fear revealed. Her childish wish to dispose of her mother so that she could have her father all to herself had caused her intense guilt. Terror that the strength of her jealousy would overwhelm her mother had made Martina bury her 'bad' wish deep in her subconscious.

Once she was able to confront this childish part of herself, her fear and guilt were reduced to manageable proportions and reparation to her mother became a possibility.

Psychotherapy is by no means an instant panacea. A long period of examining their own and each other's needs lay ahead of Robert and Martina but, without this vital first step, Martina would not have been able to see her way ahead. In the light of what she had started to learn about herself and her early relationship with her parents, she was able to see what it was that was missing from her own marriage.

It is ironic that crossing emotional and sexual boundaries, rather than drawing us together, also drives us apart. As a child Martina had longed for closer contact with her elusive father. Competition with her mother over her father's love had led to an unsatisfactory link between mother and daughter that was only reforged in adulthood. That left 'unfinished business' with her father which Martina had tried to regenerate and resolve in her relationship with Robert. There was also an underlying fear that her needs might overpower his and that he would try and escape through emotional withdrawal as her father had done from her mother.

In this way Robert's behaviour had corroborated her deep fear of her own voracious emotional appetite. The message Martina had received was that neither her parents nor Robert nor anyone else could ever cope with her longing for intimacy. Not surprisingly, this had left her feeling desolate and depressed. To a certain extent her subconscious suppositions had been correct. Robert was indeed scared of intimacy – which is by no means rare among men or women. We may not always be aware of it, but it remains a common factor in many marital difficulties and is yet another aspect of the phenomenon of 'unfinished business'.

In the developing intimacy between lovers many echoes may

be set off in certain situations that may remind us of what we prefer to forget. For a man who has struggled to become separate from his mother and assert his masculine independence, close contact with another female may threaten his sense of self. He may easily react with an emotional retreat as Robert had done from Martina, thus repeating the family history she feared so much. Robert had an unconscious dread of being 'swallowed up' by the bottomless well of Martina's loneliness. His habit of psychologically holding her at arm's length simultaneously frustrated and increased her desire for more intimacy. At the same time her reaction confirmed his fears of not being able to give her what she wanted.

Robert dared not reveal the love he felt for Martina because he subconsciously associated it with weakness. It was, he believed, the antithesis of the qualities of strength and power that had attracted her in the first place. He felt that by supplying the emotional support Martina needed he would also remove both the foundations of his self-identity and her reason for loving him. There seemed to be no way out of this emotional impasse.

The discoveries they had made both about themselves and each other clarified their perception of themselves as a couple. Martina and Robert gradually began to realize the potential for change and growth within their relationship. Without the presence of a neutral third party Robert would have felt incapable of articulating his feelings:

If we had been on our own discussions would quickly have deteriorated into rows that led nowhere. Instead I actually had to sit down and really listen, something Martina had been pleading with me to do for years. I have a lot of guilt for what I must have put her through, but I am certainly going to try and make it up to her now.

Martina now sees the possibility of real happiness ahead with Robert and their son:

I am no longer caught up in the past but free to look to our future together. Now that I can see where we were both going wrong I think we can get over our problems. Knowing that Robert is really 'there' for me after all has made me feel secure for the first time in my life.

101

Both Martina and Robert are now involved in the difficult and lengthy process of settling their 'unfinished business'. They have recognized their needs and their love for each other and are trying to balance their newfound knowledge with their mutual independence. To be able to merge and yet simultaneously retain our autonomy is no easy task but struggling towards its realization brings its own rewards in the form of individual growth.

Unfinished business is not necessarily always left over from childhood. The turbulence of the teenage years can build up its own backlog of interrupted trauma. Present loves, hates and jealousies sometimes have far more to do with retrospective experience than we realize. Re-examination of our emotional records may well be required before we are able to distinguish between the scar of an old wound and a more recent injury.

Deborah did not enjoy her late teens. She was the unfortunate victim of both acne and a temporary obesity and her ego suffered as much from the sniggers of her so-called friends as from the casual cruelty of adolescent males – until she met Stephen. Stephen was the epitome of the teenage heart-throb and he worked hard to maintain the image. An inbuilt awareness of his singular style plus a certain sarcastic charm marked him out as a natural winner where women were concerned. No one, least of all the girl herself, understood why he selected Deborah from the swarm of adulatory females that seemed always to surround him. Deborah understandably adored him; her ego expanded as her skin cleared and her waistline shrank. On her eighteenth birthday they made love for the first and last time. Sexy, suave Stephen was unable to maintain an erection. Since Deborah had had very little sexual experience she interpreted this as a sign of rejection. Stephen's embarrassment prevented him from rescuing her from her misapprehension. It was easier to let Deborah take the 'blame'.

The effect on Deborah of this ending to her first affair was devastating. She was immune both to the condolences of her friends and the cliché-ridden comforts offered up by her parents. She simply withdrew, quietly and politely, from day-to-day life, lying on her bed and refusing either to study, socialize, eat or sleep. Eventually her mother called in their local GP who prescribed a short course of tranquillizers and advised leaving her 'to get over it in her own way'.

Deborah's way was to dig a deep hole in her subconscious, stuff all her emotional suffering into it and emerge as if refreshed and back to normal. Her parents were naturally very pleased to see her apparent recovery. She started going out again although studiously avoiding anywhere which might involve meeting Stephen. The mere mention of his name was enough to submerge her in gloom. He eventually contacted her again and suggested that they get together again 'as friends'. Surprisingly, Deborah accepted this with alacrity, even going so far as to tolerate the presence of a succession of Stephen's new girlfriends but, deep down inside, Deborah's sexual self-confidence was in fragments. She was in danger of falling apart at any moment. Liaisons with likely young males were short-lived since they all quickly sensed Deborah's obsession with her former lover. Stephen knew it too but chose to ignore it. With one word he could have restored her self-esteem, but the loss of his own was too high a price to pay.

To the relief of those who cared for Deborah, university intervened to separate her from Stephen. As Deborah started to build a relationship with a fellow student named David the memory of Stephen finally seemed to slide into the past where it belonged. Except for one extremely important aspect of their life together David seemed happy. He began to notice that each time they made love Deborah would become depressed. She could not explain why but admitted he was right. Since David at first interpreted this as a rejection of his sexual advances, Deborah's unfinished business with Stephen was still powerful enough to pose a threat to her future.

Fortunately, Deborah at this point decided to do something to try and sort out her confused sexual feelings. She attended a workshop on women and sexuality where in the 'safe' atmosphere of a group of supportive women she felt able to talk through her early sexual experiences. The idea that Stephen's impotence might have been 'his' problem rather than anything to do with her sexual attractiveness had never occurred to

Deborah. The possibility cast light on that bit of the past she thought she had so effectively buried. She felt able to confront her feelings for the first time. The fact that Stephen had not been able to make love to her was no longer greatly significant. She could allow herself to forget it and be happy with David:

I kept thinking, 'it doesn't matter any more. I am free of those fears from the past. The only thing that is important is that David and I can show our love for each other.'

Deborah's phantom of sexual inadequacy had finally been exorcized.

Discharging unfinished business demands both courage and time. We need to tie up all the emotional loose ends before we can feel free to make further progress towards maturity. Of course, not every woman's emotional back-log is so heavy that it requires psychotherapy or professional counselling. Sometimes a simple chat with a close friend can provide a solution to transitory sadness. However, when shadows from the past constantly interfere with present happiness, it is time to turn around and work out what went wrong. If we cannot do it alone it makes sense to seek outside help. We don't have to become the hapless victims of our own emotional history for ever. Unravelling yesterday's problems will often help us to understand those we have today.

7

Work and self-worth

The Gordian Knot of a seemingly insoluble feminine dilemma has been cut. The technical and social developments of the last few decades have given women the opportunity to integrate their two interests in Home and Work ... No longer need women forego the pleasures of one sphere in order to enjoy the satisfaction of the other. The best of both worlds has come within their grasp, if only they reach out for it.

(*Women's Two Roles*, Myrdal and Klein)

This was the overwhelmingly optimistic view of a sociological study published in 1956. It was also very misleading. The perfectly run 'home' pictured here appears to involve no effort on the woman's part or, if it does, she is assumed to derive gratification from doing it all singlehanded. 'Work' is somewhere she goes to fulfil herself intellectually – there is no mention of the screaming boredom of a factory production line or of there being any financial necessity to go to work at all.

Let's face facts – many women take on the most menial of tasks for a pathetic pittance of a wage in order to supplement an inadequate family income. Their contribution is not for personal satisfaction or self-fulfilment but simply vital to economic survival. Ask them if they feel they are getting the best of both worlds. The dilemma identified here by those smug fifties sociologists is confined to women who are sufficiently highly educated or skilled to command a high salary or, alternatively, to those whose husband's financial support liberates them from their luxurious but lonely homes to enjoy the social stimulus of an intellectually undemanding job.

'Work' is not an intrinsically pleasant or rewarding pastime.

The daily grind of labour can be dull and dispiriting for both sexes but the politics of the workplace are almost universally male-orientated – men from the shop floor to the boardroom fight fiercely for the next step up the celestial ladder of which salary forms only a part. They simultaneously conspire to preserve the system that manipulates them with such military dexterity. Men are promoted, demoted or discarded purely in terms of performance, while women still suffer the ignominy of being selected on grounds of their sexual desirability.

By the end of an average working week an employee who happens to be both wife and mother can easily be reduced to a state of complete mental and physical exhaustion. For many women life can seem like one long worry about resources of energy, time and money. Like Alice's white rabbit they clock-watch constantly as they ricochet between supermarket and school gates in a futile attempt to keep offspring, freezer and store-cupboards constantly stocked up with food.

All this effort is met with precious little recompense in terms of either emotional or job satisfaction. Employers and family alike can seem only too ready to criticize at the first sign of a malfunction. Yet it is to this exhausting treadmill that so many women aspire. Feminist theory, to some extent, has let women down here. Far from challenging the male value-system of work and self-worth, it has simply demanded (and to some extent won) an entry ticket for women into it. Exploitation by a single male at home has merely given way to exploitation by many others at work.

Sociologists of the eighties have tossed aside the rose-tinted spectacles of their predecessors – the statistics bear out the truth that women still come off worse in terms of the amount of work done (both in and outside the home) and the rewards of prestige, wealth or power they might gain in return.

The Social Trends report of 1987 (an annual 'state of the nation' update prepared by the Central Statistical Office) reveals that women working full time still earn proportionately less than men and perform the least pleasant jobs. As if this were not enough, they are sixty-six times more likely to be the partner who takes time off from work if the children are sick.

Not surprisingly, since we do eighty-eight times as much washing and ironing, we have nine hours less free time a week than men.

Although nearly 50 per cent of women now also work outside the home, house-management is still generally assumed (by both sexes) to be primarily the responsibility of the woman.

After twenty years of so-called liberation there is a depressing irony about the major areas of our lives over which we actually have control. Women are now far more likely to sue for divorce than their husbands (67,000 in 1971 had risen to 185,000 in 1985) and are becoming increasingly dependent on cigarettes. It is hard to avoid having a mental image of an overworked, chain-smoking harridan, not quite the new Amazon that Betty Friedan had in mind all those years ago. Reports like these serve to remind us of something we are all too aware of in our day-to-day life: the shortfall between women's expectations and the likelihood of their fulfilment.

Convincing signs of progress are rare and confined mainly to a privileged few. It is sad but true that those that do succeed are often forced to do so on the backs of their less fortunate sisters. Women must be wealthy before they can afford both the luxury of a structured career plus the adequate domestic support without which it would be impossible. We are beginning to discover the truth we half-suspected all along – that Superwoman isn't quite so super after all. Even Shirley Conran now feels that, like a female Frankenstein, she may have been responsible for creating a monster beyond her control.

What choice do we really have? Women still cannot choose to have it all. Charting the future may no longer be a stark choice between career or marriage but many still have to face the far crueller dilemma of deciding which to put first – their careers or their children.

Having completely unrealistic expectations of ourselves can ultimately lead only to disappointment and self-disdain. We can try our best at personal fulfilment, but we must beware of destroying ourselves in the process. The first and most important question must remain 'Who am I doing this for?' If the answer is 'For myself – I want to have a high-flying career/happy home (ideally with the added bonus of an exotic sex life)', then fair enough.

She who dares may win but there are many women who, having grown up with feminism and some of its promises, force themselves to act out a role for which they are miscast. Women are not all made in the same mould. Maturity must involve discovering who we really are and following it through, despite the dictates of society or pressure from friends. It is we who have to live with the consequences of our life-choices. No one is going to care or congratulate us upon our success or otherwise in conforming to some contemporary role-model which will in any case be revived by our children as they come to make those same decisions about whom they wish to emulate.

Barbara, at thirty-eight, was a busy paediatrician in a large London teaching hospital. With two children, James and Clare, both under five, she depended upon a succession of continually unreliable home-helpers and au pairs. Her husband Jerry, also a paediatrician at the same hospital, was understanding and supportive but Barbara still felt that the major burden of domestic responsibility fell on her shoulders:

Jerry helped all right. But that's just it. He didn't see it as being part of his domain. It always felt as though he was doing me a favour rather than sharing a joint problem. I had to be ruthless to succeed. Even when Clare got a severe ear infection I had to leave her to go and look after someone else's sick child. It was absurd. We didn't need the money that desperately but I had been brought up to be a high-achiever and just couldn't stop competing.

As the pressures piled on Barbara became more and more remote from her family. Resentment and guilt presented themselves in equal proportions as she tried to divide her life successfully between home and hospital. Eventually Barbara came to the conclusion she could no longer carry on leading a dual existence without enjoying either part of her life as she had used to:

I saw the children as preventing me from fulfilling my medical aspirations when I was at home, and my work stopping me from being a

108

good mother when I was at the hospital. I had to talk to someone to sort out my mixed-up feelings.

Barbara chose to confide in an elderly woman doctor now close to retirement. With three failed marriages and a corresponding number of grown children behind her, Margaret had had a great deal of experience to draw upon:

Her first question was so obvious in its simplicity that I was amazed I had never asked it of myself before. Did I want to work outside the home? If so, why? I realized that I had never analysed my reasons for working. Jerry and I had just assumed that I would carry on working after the children were born because I had a professional career, and because all our friends did. That was when I decided to take a break for a couple of years.

The gap has fortunately not affected Barbara's career. She now says she knows she made the right decision in focussing all her energies on her family for a few years. She also knows she was lucky in having a career which fulfilled her idealistic and feminist aspirations as well as sustaining the potentially damaging effects of interrupted work experience.

Few women further down the educational or economic scale can draw the same rewards from working outside the home. As a cleaner in the same hospital where Barbara was a doctor, thirty-eight-year-old Linda finds little personal satisfaction or life-enhancement from her low-status job. What she does get is pay, and the company of other women like herself. Having suffered from depression as a result of her husband Pete's redundancy and her own isolation at home with small children, work seemed the obvious way out. This does not mean that any work is automatically an instant cure for mental distress. All it signifies is that, in our society to date, work outside the home is seen as having a higher status than that done within, and that being alone all day can become intellectually and emotionally stultifying. Linda:

I couldn't really say I enjoyed my job. I'm exhausted most of the time. But we can have a laugh together, and it's much better than being on my own all day. I don't want to end up down at the doctor's again. But I do mind the fact that it's still me who does all the shopping, cooking, washing and cleaning. I do the same hours that Pete does now he's back in work, but I still have to come home and cook. Even when I was working and he wasn't he never used to get the supper. If I could be back at home and still see all my friends I think I'd be all right.

In Linda's case it is the lack of social contact that encourages emotional disturbance and loss of self-esteem rather than the absence of employment outside the home.

It is far easier to clock on and off as we are told than to structure our own day. It is frightening to be alone but it is also an ultimately unavoidable factor of human existence. Going out to work masks the underlying anxiety we all experience at the thought of having to fall back on our own resources. It is also something that we all eventually have to come to terms with, whether through choice or the enforced isolation of motherhood, redundancy or retirement. For all of us there must ultimately come a day when there is no longer anyone further up the ladder than ourselves to tell us what to do. For this reason it is important to decide right now whether we are really doing what we want to do or what we feel we 'ought' to be doing.

8

The power to change ourselves – the power to change the world

Over the last ten years the popular psychology industry has provided more than enough encouragement for women to indulge in introspection and solipsistic self-analysis. I would add quickly that this is not the purpose of this book. Acres of women's magazines and feature pages have been produced, inumerable books and worthy pamphlets have been published, all exhorting us to achieve 'excellence' – at work, in the kitchen, in the gym, in bed, wherever, but the message that comes across is a crassly and openly critical one. We are asked to assess ourselves constantly not just in terms of our physical attraction (although this is the predominant message) but also in our ability to 'cope', to be 'serene', to be anything but a neurotic cow.

We are then left worrying like crazy that that is just what we are – neurotic, anorexic, too fat, too thin, too old, too anything – and bad mothers to boot.

All this self-dissection may or may not be a good idea but one fundamental point is often missed in the process: self-analysis is only useful if it functions in two important ways. Firstly, it should help us to recognize what might be wrong with the way we are. Secondly, it should promote in us a desire to change as the simple and natural expression of a desire to improve the quality of life for ourselves and our families. The strength of that desire to change is a major factor in our success.

Success in this sense means acquiring the ability to come to terms with reality and its limitations. Some people are lucky enough to be born with it but it can also be learned. However we

111

finally attain it there is no doubt that this life-skill is an integral part both of personal maturity and of making and maintaining successful relationships with others. We have to learn to accept the world the way it is if we are not to waste our lives howling at the moon.

Having accepted the world the way it is, can we accept ourselves and the possibility of change? If we are unhappy the internal sovereignty of our own identities can and should be exercised to change our condition. We don't have to stay trapped at the mercy of our own unhappiness – all we need is the motivation to escape from the role of victim, to abandon self-pity and start planning how to change both what we don't like about ourselves and what may be wrong with the way we live.

It's no use continually railing against the cruel destiny that caused us to be born women in the first place. If we feel perpetually exhausted or dogged by depression and anxiety it is time to stand back and reassess the way we are running our lives. It's time to make changes. Reorganizing the day so that there is at least some space allocated purely for personal relaxation in any form, be it a favourite sport or simply slumping in an armchair, is one positive way of breaking a cycle of self-punishing routines. Feeling guilty does not come into it – a bitter and resentful wife and mother benefits nobody in the long term, least of all herself.

We cannot change our lives in isolation from those around us. We have to start looking at the way others' behaviour interacts with our own so that we can see why things sometimes go wrong when we don't mean them to. Unhappy people are often so over-subjective that they simply overlook the fact that other people are different from them and they forget to make simple accommodations. Different desires and viewpoints deserve equal consideration and respect. If we feel that we could be happier if only our husbands/partners/children/work colleagues behaved differently towards us, we have first to look at what it is they do which upsets us so much and, secondly, obvious as it may sound, to tell them about it.

This simple act is very important – poor communication can be a problem in the most loving of families, creating a log-jam of bitterness and resentment built on silence over the years, waiting to burst.

112

Winning back control

All of us have a degree of control over our lives and we don't need to keep on making the same mistakes once we have the will to break free of them. Reason is our greatest ally. Looking at personal problems objectively and analysing both why they happened and what practical steps we can take to prevent them arising again is a useful and quickly effective way of proving our personal strength. Once this power has been confirmed by practical application, self-confidence will start to build up again because it is positively reinforced by success.

Before embarking on a programme of personal change you need to work out a sensible plan of campaign, distinguishing between which aspects of self and which of lifestyle are causing the problems. The two will undoubtedly interact but there is no use altering one without the other. Getting to know yourself is not as easy as it may sound, but trying to remould yourself to someone else's measurements is as frustrating as it is futile. Being happy 'in your own skin' is essential.

So how does one begin this difficult task of self-identification? Simply writing down lists of what you want to change about the way you act and why can be a surprisingly effective means of getting started and pinning down free-floating anxieties. List making can help to show up your strengths and weaknesses more clearly but it is not as simple as that. Personality is constantly changing. It develops as a combination of inherited characteristics and interactive experience. As a result, it is constantly elusive, and the best you can hope for is an intermittent freeze-frame of yourself showing the recurrence of certain traits. Once this individual pattern has been recognized you can start to separate out these essential qualities by writing down a number of abilities (in any field) that you feel you possess (as many as you like). Follow this with a list of social skills and then study them. Try to be as objective as possible before asking a friend or a close family member (without showing them the personal list) to describe you, using the same format. Make sure that they understand how important it is to be truthful.

This simple test should make the shortfall between how you

really are and how you would like to be very clear. If you're one of those people who tend to run themselves down you may also receive a few pleasant surprises as others identify additional attributes you may not have considered.

The next step is to look at your lifestyle. Write down all the adolescent ambitions that you can recall from the past and match them up with the present. Are there many deviations in direction, mistakes or disappointments to be admitted to? If there are think next what could be done to put them right, and how to set about doing it as soon as possible. Basic personality traits cannot be transformed but they can be controlled once recognized. Regaining this sense of control promotes self-confidence and encourages further progress.

Don't expect instant results. The process is a tough and demanding one and occasional setbacks are to be expected – we may fall down almost as many snakes as we scale ladders but, ironically, by the time the transformation is complete, the former self is conveniently forgotten. The psyche seems to have an inbuilt safety device for blocking out the unacceptable, and old anxieties are mercifully difficult to recall. Like recalling physical pain, we remember the existence of worries rather than what it was like to live through them.

An effective strategy is to tackle the enemy in two stages. Firstly, imagine how different life will be when the problem has been eradicated. Start thinking of yourself as a person without a worry. Secondly, start acting the role until it eventually becomes a reality. Convincing yourself is really your hardest task, once you believe in yourself others will soon start to follow.

The power to change the world

Changing ourselves is obviously only a part of the answer to our problems as women. Society as a whole must take much of the responsibility for the fact that it is possible to compare a contemporary woman's life to a game of snakes and ladders.

My monthly postbag gives evidence of a multitide of women clamouring for release from the confinement of their own particular misery. Something is still rotten in the state of sexual politics and the life of the family in a period when the statistics for rape, incest and child-abuse are so rapidly rising. However, the picture is not a uniformly black one. We all know how good it can be when we get relationships right, and how vital close human contact can be to our emotional survival. Introspective retreat is not an answer to unhappiness. Avoiding intimacy ultimately diminishes us as it deprives us of the opportunity for all-round fulfilment. We owe it to ourselves to try to get it right. What often prevents us is both an individual and a race memory of our previous powerlessness. Inhibited by history, we hold each other back from breaking free but changing the nature of women's lives remains an exciting and challenging possibility. It is the essential clause for inclusion in any future draft peace treaty between the sexes. We have to start believing that we have the ability as women to change what makes us unhappy on a universal as well as a personal level. The power to influence events is bought at a price – the personal assumption of responsibility. Suddenly the buck stops here and we are all going to have to do something about it.

Social change is always easier to identify retrospectively. The slow striptease of sexual stereotyping was an agonizingly long act but now we are beginning to get down to the basics. Men as well as women have suffered from the locking-in process by which we divide the sexes from birth: 'No emotions for you, mate. Ruin the concentration and the rational thought processes. Have a few practical and sporting skills instead. No need for any of that "caring" stuff either. Just build up the macho image with a knowledge of mechanics and a bit of sexual prowess and you'll do fine.' Not any more, he won't. Past and present sexual role-models just don't work any more. We are going to have to develop new ones if we are to stem the rising tide of female dissatisfaction with the emotional input of the opposite sex. Now that women have won their way into the traditionally male preserves it is time that men woke up to the pay-offs as well as the drudgery of the domestic domain. If childrearing could become a genuine dual responsibility the difficulties of separation and self-identification from the same sex parent could be considerably relieved. There would be a previously unknown symmetry to psychological development. We have only to look at the ways in which both sexes suffer under the present regime to see that it is time for a new equality in parenthood. This would remove much of the intolerable pressure currently imposed on women. Traditional formulas for family life no longer work. Experimentation with new ways of relating to and living with those we love is an essential part of the process of trying to create the new Eden. The trauma of divorce followed by the strains of single or step-parenthood offer a bleak alternative to those who refuse to allow for change or development. People are no longer prepared to put up with second-best and prefer to cut loose rather than remain confined to a partner who constrains them. As women expect more from themselves, so have they come to demand more equality of emotional commitment and practical support from their male partners. Ultimatums demand action. Men can no longer pretend that feelings don't matter. Before we women can claim true sovereignty over our own emotional health, we must rectify our lop-sided liaisons with the opposite sex. The satisfaction both sexes can get from self-fulfilment in work should not be a substitute for the happiness to be found in forging strong links with those we love.

Experiments in new ways of living together may not always work out but they are at least an attempt to get things right. Many designs for living may have to be scrapped before we finally find the new prototype. The important difference between those and former models lies in the additional skill of their designers. Feminism has made a major contribution to our knowledge of our own emotional history and we must now incorporate this new information into any blueprint for the future of the family.

How would such a model operate in practice and in what ways could it lighten women's emotional workload? An awareness of sexual politics is essential. An adolescent girl growing up in the atmosphere of a household in which both parents were seen as happy and self-fulfilled in every area of their lives, including the ability to express their mutual emotional dependence, would not be as likely to suffer from the sort of psychological stresses examined in this book. 'Mother' would no longer be a role-model for feelings of inadequacy, guilt or low self-esteem. Seeing as much of her father as of her mother would make separation and self-identification that much easier. She would not necessarily be seeking a second mother in her first relationship with a man, neither would she be expecting men to make up for something missing in her own life. If and when she chose to have children of her own, she would have the security of knowing that her partner would be willing to share all the domestic as well as the emotional responsibilities that maternity brings with it, and that motherhood would not impose a threat to her career structure in the outside world at any time.

Likewise, the ability to do well at work would no longer induce feelings of guilt or betrayal. Success wouldn't have to cast any shadows on her life. Individual achievement would be a cause of mutual celebration, devoid of jealousy or resentment since neither partner would have regrets for what they might have relinquished either on the home or the work front. Feelings of self-worth would thrive on the fertile soil of all-round fulfilment and there would no longer be any need for such treacherous props as alcohol or tranquillizers.

As she grew older there would be no need to feel afraid for loss of status since she would have gained love and respect in her youth for something more enduring than her looks. The death of a spouse would not pull the plug on her own personality since this would no longer be based on the premise that women derive their identity from men. Would this Utopia work in practice? There is no reason why it shouldn't if both men and women are willing to work together to achieve it.

All around us women are searching for ways out of their dilemma. The 'New Man' is willing to take a more active part in the role of parenting, while some women are choosing either to forgo having a family altogether or to bring up a child without the support of a father. Something positive must emerge from all this experimentation. These are not purely practical issues. Women are playing to win but they are no longer willing to risk the loss of their autonomy just to take part in the game.

No great transitions are going to take place overnight. It may take several generations before any really new patterns start to emerge. Many experiments will be tried and will fail; what works for some won't work for all, but we may find ourselves coming to some sort of consensus about the ways in which we interconnect.

Does individual autonomy automatically exclude the possibility of love on equal terms? That has certainly been the pervasive spirit of our age. Autonomy of the self has come to be regarded as sacrosanct. Large parts of our culture view emotional ties as betraying our prime responsibility to ourselves – just look at soap-opera plots, for example, with all those monstrous egos colliding with each other in a series of power-plays dressed up as affairs. The fallout from the 'me-generation' still accepts as a divine creed: 'Thou shalt not suffer another to intrude on thy space'.

Willing to tread on one another's shoulders to reach the top, the new upward climbers of either gender prefer not to encumber themselves with emotional commitment either to people or causes. Future generations of women are not going to get very far towards all-round fulfilment by simply making themselves more like men. We would be stepping into a very lonely and bleak world indeed if we were to lose the nurturing skills of both sexes at one stroke. Men are also going to have to change their perspective on life, to open themselves up to the possibility of self-exploration and the expression of their personal weaknesses and anxieties as well as new found strengths. Equal divisions of childcare and domestic routine could result in a reassessment of the value of such work. It could at last be seen in its true light as an essential and valuable contribution to everyday life rather than casually dismissed or exaggeratedly exalted as an end in itself. Women would no longer feel the need to nag or scold those around them since the running of the house would be seen as a collective effort instead of a burden falling on their shoulders alone.

The switch from sole responsibility for the home would have to be accompanied by a restructuring of the outside world of work, otherwise self-esteem would drop to even lower levels as women experienced a temporary sense of loss for the only sphere in which, though at present exploited, they still hold a certain degree of power. Both sexes will take time to come to terms with the bartering of their former roles and the ensuing feelings of inadequacy and anxiety as the emphasis on certain areas shifts between them. Growing up in a household where parents both go out into the world and work within the home would affect the psychological development of boy and girl alike. They would benefit equally from learning to detect and comfort each other's emotional distress, and would have experience of the good and bad aspects of people as individuals rather than as representatives of an alien sex.

How we are to achieve this ideal state of affairs is another question. The work begun by the women's movement must carry on but with a change of tactic. We must end hostilities and start putting forward positive peace proposals which can be expanded and worked upon to the benefit of both sexes. With a strong sense of our own self-worth and the freedom of economic independence we will stand a much better chance of finding happiness in an equal-terms partnership. Wishful thinking must be translated into practical action. Ending the traditional trade-off of economic for emotional security between male and female is the first step. Only then can we be sure that our commitment is formed on the basis of love rather than fear. Marriage was never meant to be run along the lines of a Mafia protection racket. In the twentieth century marriage has become so debased that many couples dispense with it altogether. Any new medium of exchange needs to reflect the shared interests of both parties. Neither side can afford to lose what the other has to offer in the way of mutual support, intimacy and dependency if the snakes are to be avoided and those ladders finally scaled.

Where To Get Help
When Things Go Wrong

Abortion

The threat of an unwanted pregnancy can throw you into an emotional turmoil just at the time when you need to take one of the most important decisions of your life. Don't delay – your first priority is to find out if you really are pregnant so that there can be enough time for an informed and clear-headed decision.

Any of the following symptoms can indicate pregnancy: a missed period, swollen or sensitive breasts, nausea, the frequent desire to urinate.

Take an early morning urine sample to your doctor (ask if this may mean a delay in obtaining a result) or Family Planning clinic (this will involve paying a small fee but means you will also have access to sympathetic professional counselling and practical information on obtaining an abortion). Alternatively, you can get the test done at your local chemist or buy a DIY test to do at home. Results are fairly reliable but it is always sensible to follow up a negative test with a repeat (preferably by a doctor or clinic) a fortnight later, especially if symptoms persist.

TALKING IT THROUGH
Whatever your immediate reaction to a positive result, don't act on impulse and don't feel you must punish yourself by trying to cope singlehanded. Try to find either a trustworthy friend or a professional counsellor with whom to discuss the situation. It is a good way of reflecting your true feelings and reassuring yourself that you have made the 'right' decision for you at this moment in your life. Examining all the various options open to you will also help to relieve you from feeling trapped or forced into a decision.

Ideally, a GP should be able to provide nonjudgmental counselling to pregnant women but in practice many find that their religious or moral attitudes get in the way of their objectivity. If you feel that your doctor would not be helpful, you could contact the British Pregnancy Advisory Service (BPAS) or the Pregnancy Advisory Service (PAS), both of which charge a small fee, or the Brook Advisory Centre (voluntary donation).

Termination can be carried out under the terms of the Abortion Act 1967 if two registered medical practitioners agree that:
1. Your life is at greater risk by continuing the pregnancy than by terminating it;
2. Your physical or mental health is more likely to be injured by continuing the pregnancy than by terminating it;
3. The physical or mental health of any existing children is more likely to be injured by continuing with the pregnancy than by terminating it;
4. There is a reasonable chance that the baby may be abnormal or deformed.
(This is applicable only to England and Wales. Abortion is illegal in Northern Ireland and the Republic. In Scotland a consultant's letter is required before referral for termination is possible.)

Married women do not need their husband's consent but girls under the age of sixteen need the consent of one parent.

WHERE TO GO
If your GP is not sympathetic you can try to find one who is. You can also ring local hospitals to see a consultant. The advisory agencies already mentioned may be able to tell you which hospitals to apply to.

Make sure when you get an appointment that the interval between appointment and termination is not going to put you over the fourteen-week limit as this would involve a lengthier operation with a higher degree of risk.

Private sector
Going private guarantees you a quick operation but beware of profit-making private clinics without recommendation since your welfare may not be their primary consideration.

The non-profit-making registered charities have won themselves wide respect for providing women with emotional as well as practical support before, during and after this period of intense personal stress.

After six weeks and up to fourteen weeks abortion can be safely and simply carried out by a method known as vacuum aspiration. This means that the contents of the womb are removed by suction. You can request day-care for this operation which is done under anaesthetic.

After fourteen weeks termination is carried out by induction. Artificial hormones are given by injection to cause the womb to contract in exactly the same way as it would during labour. This is obviously a longer process and may involve two or three days in hospital. A medical check-up six weeks after the operation is usual to make sure that everything has returned to normal.

If you also feel you need to talk to someone about your feelings after the operation, BPAS, PAS and the Women's Therapy Centre all offer counselling.

British Pregnancy Advisory Service, Austy Manor, Wootton Wawen, Solihull, West Midlands, B95 6BX (05642 3225) Ring or write for a list of local branches.
London: 7, Belgrave Road, London, SW1 1QB

Pregnancy Advisory Service, 11–13, Charlotte Street, London W1P 1HD (01 637 8962)

Brook Advisory Centre, 233 Tottenham Court Road, London W1P 9AE (01 323 1522)

Release Emergency Service, 169 Commercial Street, London, E1 6BW (01 603 8654) Provides 24-hour nationwide advice on abortion referral as well as drugs and related problems. Also 01 377 5905 (10am–6pm, Mon-Fri)

Adolescence

It's not so easy to know where to go for help with the numerous and often embarrassing worries and fears that can surround you in the teenage years. It's great if you feel you can talk to your parents or to your GP confidentially. If not, contact one of the organizations listed below. Counsellors will be understanding, uncritical and experienced in talking to young people.

National Association for Young Person's Counselling and Advisory Service (NAYPCAS), 17–23 Albion Street, Leicester LE1 6GD (0533 558763) A national information centre providing counselling, advice and information for young people.

New Grapevine, 416 St John Street, London EC1V 4NJ (01 278 9147) Tuesday 10.30–12.30 Wednesday 2.30–6.30 A national network of young people's advisory centres, offering a birth control service, pregnancy testing and abortion counselling.

Agoraphobia

Contrary to popular belief this distressing condition is not confined to fear of 'open spaces' but is a generalized panic about facing all sorts of day-to-day situations from stopping at a petrol station to shopping in the local supermarket. Eventually the settings of previous attacks themselves become the trigger that sparks off another and the victim becomes caught in an escalating cycle of almost permanent anxiety.

TREATMENT AVAILABLE
Approach your GP first. S/he may or may not suggest a short course of tranquillizers to get you over a crisis. S/he can also refer you for specialist treatment if you are lucky enough to live near one of the small number of hospitals providing agoraphobic programme therapy.

Hypnosis
Won't work alone. Only provides short-term relief unless combined with learned techniques of stress control. Beware unqualified practitioners unless personally recommended, it is safer either to get in touch with the British Hypnotherapy Association, who keep a list of registered practitioners, or ask your doctor to refer you to the British Society of Medical and

126

Dental Hypnosis, c/o Ms M. Samuels, 42 Links Road, Ashtead, Surrey KT21 2HJ

Acupuncture
Technique by which needles are inserted into the body at certain points as part of a healing or preventative process. Practitioners believe this works by altering the flow of energy to different parts of the body. High degree of success in the treatment of some anxiety states so it's probably worth a try where conventional medicine appears to have failed. Again, avoid unqualified practitioners by consulting either of the two following organizations:

The British Acupuncture Association and Register, 34, Alderney Street, London, SW1 4EU (01 834 1012/3353)

The Traditional Acupuncture Society, 11 Grange Park, Stratford-upon-Avon, Warwickshire, CV37 6XH (0789 298798)

Homeopathy
A branch of 'holistic' or 'whole person' medicine. Illness is regarded as a sign of disharmony within the individual so the treatment is directed at the patient rather than the symptoms. Most chemists now stock a variety of simple safe 'herbal' remedies but it is advisable to consult a homeopathic practitioner before experimenting without sufficient knowledge of the subject.

British Homeopathic Association, 27A Devonshire Street, London W1N 1RJ (01 935 2163)

SELF-HELP
Undoubtedly the safest and most effective solution, with the advantage that it puts you in touch with the support of fellow sufferers.

Open Door Association, c/o 447, Pensby Road, Heswall, Wirral, Merseyside L61 9PQ (051 648 2022) An information service for agoraphobics. Newsletter, records, cassettes and books prepared by medical personnel. You may remain anonymous or be put in touch with other members in your area.

The Phobics Society, 4 Cheltenham Road, Chorlton-cum-Hardy, Manchester M21 1QN (061 881 1937) Network throughout the country where problems can be discussed. Provides printed information.

National Association for Mental Health (MIND), 22 Harley Street, London W1N 2ED (01 637 0741) Always someone available to give specialist advice and information.

AIDS – Acquired Immunodeficiency Syndrome HTLV-III or HIV

AIDS attacks the immune system which protects the body from infection. This means that even a cough or cold can develop into a potentially life-threatening disease and once the virus begins to spread it is a virtual death sentence. The incubation period can be anything from six months to over five years, although catching AIDS does not automatically mean that one will develop symptoms. It was not officially recognized until 1981 so the facts about it are not yet fully understood.

HOW IT IS CAUGHT
There are only a few ways in which AIDS may be transmitted: by intimate sexual contact, by intravenous drug users who share infected needles, by blood transfusion (blood is now screened in the UK to detect HIV contamination). It is also possible for a mother to pass the disease to her baby either in the womb or at the time of birth.

HOW TO AVOID IT
No risk   Solo masturbation
               Massage away from the genital area

Low risk   Mutual masturbation
               Dry kissing
               Body rubbing

Medium risk   Wet kissing

Fellatio ('Sucking')
Urination ('Watersport' external only)
Anilingus ('rimming' i.e. oral-anal sex)

High risk   Anal and vaginal intercourse (safe if condom is used)
Fisting (insertion of hand or fist into the rectum)
Sharing sex toys and needles
Any sex act which draws blood (or might involve coming into contact with open cuts or abrasions)

Do not share needles or syringes.

SYMPTOMS
Unaccountable loss of weight
Low-grade persistent fever
Dry cough
Swollen glands
Tiredness and blurred vision
White patches on tongue
Persistent itching round anal area
Persistent diarrhoea or stomach upset
Failure of cuts and infections to heal
Skin rashes and discolourations

These symptoms also occur with many other illnesses. Only if many of them occur simultaneously or you are a high-risk group (homosexual or bisexual men, drug users, haemophiliacs) or if you have recently visited a high-risk country such as Africa should you consult your doctor for a test.

If you have a test and are found to be antibody positive it will obviously have a profound effect upon your life in many ways that you may never have considered. On the practical side such simple things as obtaining life insurance suddenly become impossible, whilst on the emotional side you have to consider the full implications of being liable to transmit the disease to others in any act of penetrative intercourse. The uncertainty of not knowing whether you will develop the full-blown disease causes distress in the form of varying degrees of anxiety and depression. It is worth considering this before deciding to have the test

Counselling and advice is available at sexually-transmitted-disease clinics in every health district.

In spite of massive publicity and a government information campaign, prejudice against AIDS sufferers still exists due, mainly, to many misconceptions and ignorance of the facts. For this reason, apart from your doctor, dentist and close family it is advisable to tell as few people as possible. You do have the law on your side if you experience harassment at work or home but it is better not to risk putting yourself under any additional strain.

TREATMENT AVAILABLE

No drug has yet been found to cure HIV infection although many are currently undergoing research trials. There is also as yet no vaccine which could protect people from HIV.

Emotional support

For some people the fear of telling family and friends may cause further isolation and misery. Cases like these urgently require a confidential outlet for their anxieties.

DOH Healthline (01 981 2717, 01 980 7222 or 0345 581151)

Terrence Higgins Trust, BM AIDS, London WC1N 3XX (01 833 2971, Mon-Fri 7–10p.m. Sat-Sun 3–10p.m.) Will also put you in contact with counselling groups in your particular area.

London Lesbian and Gay Switchboard (01 837 7324) BM Switchboard, London WC1N 3XX

Haemophilia Society 123 Westminster Bridge Road, London SE1 7HR (01 928 2020)

The Standing Conference on Drug Abuse (SCODA) 1–4 Hatton Place, Hatton Garden, London EC1N 8ND (01 430 2341)

Alcoholism

One in every twelve people has a drink problem. The effects of having an alcoholic in the family are far-reaching. The social stigma attached to the illness tends to discourage sufferers from seeking help until their habit is firmly entrenched. Admitting the problem exists is an important first step towards recovery.

TREATMENT AVAILABLE

Talking to your GP can elicit a variety of responses from tranquillizers to hospital treatment, depending both on the severity of your problem and the local availability of professional help. (In extreme cases an emergency detoxification programme with or without the aid of sedation may be necessary.) Most doctors quite rightly recognize the value of the self-help sector and are able to provide information about the numerous organizations offering support both for the alcoholics themselves and their families.

Alcohol Problem Advisory Service (APAS) National Temperance Hospital, Hampstead Road, London, NW1 2LT (01 387 6354/9300 Ext. 490) Out-patients service for South Camden but will also refer those outside catchment area. Group and individual therapy.

Alcoholic Rehabilitation Centre, Woodbine Centre, Woodbine Terrace, London, E9 6RU (01 551 4481, Wednesday 7.30–10.00pm). Serves north-east London boroughs. Offers medical advice as well as individual or group therapy. Staffed by GPs, probation officers and social workers.

Women's Alcohol Centre, 254 St Paul's Road, London N1 2LJ (01 226 4581) Offers a confidential service for women. Individual and group therapy as well as practical advice, crèche facilities and some residential support. Affiliated to Alcoholics Recovery Project.

Drugs, Alcohol, Women, Nationally (DAWN), Omnibus Workspace, 39–41 North Road, London, N7 GDP (01 700 4653)

London only. Keeps list of available facilities for women. Organizes workshops on addiction and dependency as well as producing leaflets. Open meetings held every six weeks.

Al-Anon, 61 Great Dover Street, London SE1 4YF (01 403 0888, 24 hours) Provides recovery programmes for relatives and close friends of problem drinkers.

Alateen, 61 Great Dover Street, London SE1 4YF (01 403 0888, 24 hours) Offers confidential countrywide service of support and counselling for those aged between twelve and twenty whose parent, relative or close friend has a drink problem.

National Drinkwatchers Network, 200 Seagrave Road, London SW6 1RQ (01 381 3157) Offers help and advice on cutting down and controlling drinking which is beginning to cross the border-line into dependency. Tries to prevent the descent into alcoholism before it becomes a problem. Runs groups throughout Britain. Part of Alcohol Community Centres for Education, Prevention, Treatment and Research (ACCEPT).

Western Hospital, Seagrave Road, London SW6 1RZ (01 381 3115/2112) Runs treatment centres as well as counselling services for those suffering from addiction to alcohol or tranquillizers.

Allergies

Medical opinion is divided over the significance of food allergy as a factor in nervous illness but many ex-sufferers claim that changing their diet transformed their lives and it is certainly true that cutting down on caffeine can reduce nervous reactions even in nonsufferers. If you suspect this may be a part of your problem get a letter of referral from your GP to have an allergy test at the local hospital or contact one of the reputable organizations listed below. Small advertisements in the Sunday papers that offer expensive cures by such methods as hair analysis should be avoided as their ambitious claims remain unsubstantiated.

Actions Against Allergy, 43 The Downs, London SW20 8HG (01 947 5082) Offers support to allergy sufferers through local groups and by promoting research into allergies. Also keeps a booklist and a medical reference library.

National Society for Research into Allergy, PO Box 45, Hinckly, Leicester LE10 1JY (0455 635212) A research and self-help organization which also gives help on prevention. Runs a nationwide network of self-help groups.

Anorexia/bulimia nervosa

Both are tragic and health-endangering expressions of an inability to cope with either the adult world or the sufferer's own emotional reactions. There are now almost as many forms of treatment available to the victims of eating disorders as there are theories about the root cause of these distressing conditions. This can make choice about where to go for help very confusing.

TREATMENT AVAILABLE
Always consult with your own GP first. S/he can refer you to a local hospital for specialist treatment. Ten years ago you could expect drugs and forcefeeding but psychological research in this field has now led to a far more sensitive therapy-based approach. Several hospitals, notably the Maudsley, include psychotherapy as an essential component of the healing process. Can either be treated as in or out-patient depending on the severity of your particular case. May also involve family therapy. Crucial for success is the realization of why the illness was 'adopted' in the first place.

The Maudsley Hospital, Denmark Hill, London SE5
St George's Hospital, Blackshaw Road, London SW17
Atkinson Morley's Hospital, 31 Copse Hill, London SW20

Zinc supplements

Medical research is now starting to discover the importance of trace elements in the efficient functioning of our bodies. Without them, vital chemical reactions cannot take place. Zinc is a particularly significant trace element for growth and sexual development and can be lost easily through inadequate diet or stress (coffee, tea and alcohol also inhibit the body's absorption of zinc). As sufferers from both these conditions, anorexics or bulimics are more likely than most to be deficient in zinc and there is some degree of success in treatment of both illnesses through a zinc-supplemented diet.

SELF-HELP

As with all emotional illnesses success depends ultimately on the individual motivation to get better. Self-help groups have been enormously successful in the battle against anorexia and bulimia nervosa and it is certainly worth enlisting their support both for the sufferer and her family.

Anorexic Aid, The Priory Centre, 11, Priory Road, High Wycombe, Bucks HP13 6SL

Anorexics Anonymous, 45a Castlenau Road, London SW13 9RT (01 748 3994) Free counselling and advice by appointment for those suffering from anorexia, bulimia or other eating disorders.

Women's Therapy Centre, 6, Manor Gardens, N7 6LA (01 263 6200)

Anxiety

Anxiety is a natural and necessary component of everyday existence but if fear in itself starts to come between you and personal fulfilment it is time to relegate it to its proper place in life. Don't delay in asking for outside help if you need it. There is nothing to be ashamed of and the quicker you learn to deal with it the easier it is to dispel. There may be one or a million causes for its first appearance but, since chronic anxiety can easily become habit-forming, finding ways of fighting it may be more important at this stage than analysis.

Growing awareness of potential drug abuse and addiction has led both doctor and patient to a deep suspicion of the automatic resort to the prescription pad. For some people the short-term relief drugs provide may be useful in preventing the formation of a chronic pattern. Others may prefer to confront the enemy face to face in an attempt to quell their fears more quickly. Whichever you choose remember that your doctor is your best ally so keep him or her fully informed on how you want to conduct the battle. Remember that s/he is trying to help you win the way that best suits you, so if s/he offers you tranquillizers don't treat it as a temptation to cowardice or betrayal. You are simply being offered an alternative weapon against your anxiety.

Alternative therapies
See Agoraphobia for hypnosis and acupuncture addresses.

Yoga
The breathing techniques taught to students of yoga can be very beneficial in the control of tension and the reduction of stress in anxious people. Go to a qualified instructor rather than attempting to teach yourself, otherwise you may find yourself overstraining both physically and mentally. Write to the Yoga for Health Foundation, Ickwell Bury, Biggleswade, Beds SG18 9EF, who list local clubs and centres throughout the country.

SELF-HELP
Arbours Association, 41a Weston Park, London N8 NSJ (01 340 7646 Crises Centre 01 340 8125) This is a mental health charity set up to help those undergoing emotional distress. Also offers training in psychotherapy.

The Women's Therapy Centre, 6, Manor Gardens N7 6LA (01 263 6200) Send a s.a.e. for workshop programme.

Assertiveness training

We cannot force ourselves to be more confident, particularly when we are young or have been through a period of emotional stresses and strains, but there are always new ways of looking at life to be learned. Insight into past negative thought-patterns can help us to stop repeating them. There are also simple techniques which can teach us to become more assertive. If your problem is very severe you can ask your doctor to refer you for psychotherapy on the NHS but it is more than likely that the following list of organizations can assist you in helping yourself. Assertiveness training teaches you communication skills and is useful in helping you to find out what it is you really want to say as much as how to express it. Courses are run on an hourly, daily, or weekly basis.

The Redwood Women's Training Association, 83, Fordwych Road, London NW2 3TL (01 452 9261)

Women's Therapy Centre, 6 Manor Gardens, London N7 6LA (01 263 62007) Also runs workshops in assertiveness training.

Bereavement

Even though you may think you don't need it immediately it's a good idea to enlist both the practical and emotional support of others who have also been through the strain of losing someone they loved and have learnt how to begin a new life for themselves.

National Association of Widows, 1st floor, Neville House, 14, Waterloo Street, Birmingham BS2 5TX (021 643 8348)

Compassionate Friends, National Office, 6, Denmark Street, Bristol BS1 5DQ. National network providing support for those who have lost a child.

CRUSE, Cruse House, 126 Sheen Road, Richmond, Surrey,

TW9 1UR (01 940 4818/90477) Offers advice, counselling and regular newsletter for members.

Stillbirth and Neonatal Death Society (SANDS), Argyle House, 29–31, Euston Road, London NW1 2SD (01 833 2851) Network support to bereaved parents (from twenty-two weeks pregnancy to one month after birth).

Bulimia nervosa

See Anorexia

Contraception

Having a basic knowledge of contraception is vital in the avoidance of unwanted pregnancy. The dramatic impact of AIDS and the increased evidence of cervical cancer among young women means that barrier methods are now very much back in favour with both men and women.

CONDOM

The condom is simply a rubber sheath which fits over the end of the erect penis and prevents sperm from entering the vagina and fertilizing an egg. Useful in preventing the spread of AIDS as well as all other forms of sexually transmitted disease. Available free from local hospital Family Planning clinics or on sale from chemists or dispensing machines, or even garages.

DIAPHRAGM

The diaphragm (cap) is a dome of rubber which covers the cervix and works in conjunction with a spermicide to prevent sperm from entering the womb. It must be fitted either by a doctor or a specially trained nurse and should be checked every six months or sooner if there is a marked loss or gain in weight or a miscarriage. Smaller cervical caps may be more useful for women who find it difficult to use a diaphragm due to poor muscle tone. Consult your local Family Planning clinic or Brook Advisory Centre.

SPONGE

The sponge is 95 per cent effective if used properly. It acts through the release of spermicide rather than as a physical barrier. It is inserted into the vagina anything from 24 hours to just before intercourse. Not available at all Family Planning clinics but can be bought over the counter at most chemists. Not suitable for those women for whom the avoidance of pregnancy is vital as it is considered to be about twenty times less effective than the Pill.

THE PILL

This was the symbol of sexual liberation for the women of the sixties and remains the most reliable invisible method of contraception. The combined pill contains synthetic steroid hormones (oestrogen and progestogen) which together work to suppress ovulation. Most common types of combined pill are taken on twenty-one consecutive days followed by a seven-day break during which bleeding will occur. Normal patterns of menstruation should return quickly after stopping oral contraception but it is advisable to use an alternative method for a period of three months before attempting to conceive to allow accurate dating of the pregnancy.

Phasic Pills

These vary the content of hormone throughout the cycle being either bi-phasic (two different strengths) or tri-phasic (three different strengths). It is also possible to obtain ED pills (or everyday combined pills) for those who find it easier to take a pill daily without a break.

Progestogen only (or Mini) Pill

This involves less risk of the diseases associated (but not conclusively proved) of the combined pill. Taken daily they work by thickening the cervical mucus, making the womb both more difficult to penetrate and less receptive to the egg if it is fertilized. May sometimes cause irregular bleeding in some women.

Britain is now attempting to finally resolve the controversy over the contraceptive pill's potential threat to womens' health with the aid of a US-funded research programme estimated to last ten years. In the meantime thousands of women will continue to find the risk preferable to pregnancy.

IUD (INTRA-UTERINE DEVICE)

This is also very effective although not usually a first choice for most young women. Its advantages are that, once fitted, it needs no further attention from the woman herself. It consists of a small plastic device, usually wound with copper, which is passed through the cervix into the uterine cavity, usually during a period. One effect of the IUD is the prevention of the implantation of the fertilized egg within the womb. It must be inserted by a doctor and is unsuitable for women who have ever suffered from pelvic inflammation. Risks include uterine inflammation or, very rarely, perforation of the womb and ectopic (outside the womb) pregnancy. Yearly medical checks are advisable. Available free from your GP or local Family Planning clinic.

MORNING-AFTER PILL

This is for emergencies only but is useful if a sheath bursts. It involves taking an intensive dose of the combined pill within three days (or the insertion of an IUD within five days). Both procedures must be carried out under medical supervision. The high intake of oestrogen involved may cause nausea. The woman must also be willing to sign a form consenting to abortion if the method should prove ineffective. Available on prescription from your GP, Family Planning clinic or pregnancy advisory service. Always take immediate action after having unprotected sex. It has to be a first priority if you are to avoid the worry and unhappiness of an unwanted pregnancy.

STERILIZATION

This is not usually considered advisable for young people since it involves the cutting or blocking of the Fallopian tubes in women or the vas deferens in men. It is useful for couples who have completed their families but should always be regarded as permanent as in most cases attempts to reverse sterilization end in failure.

For many women who may dislike the idea of interfering with the working of their bodies or who, for religious reasons, reject mechanical forms of contraception, natural methods are an attractive if notoriously unreliable option. Measurement of body temperature and observation of changes either in the cervix itself or the cervical mucus indicate periods of possible 'safe' intercourse. Since it involves considerable self-restraint and the total commitment of both partners it is not a good method for couples who may be unsure of their feelings for one another.

Sexual fulfilment depends on our satisfaction with our method of contraception so it's worth spending time trying out what's best for you both practically and emotionally. You are far more likely to fail to use a method you are not really happy with. Any of the following organizations offer excellent medical advice and counselling as well as the fitting of any of the contraceptive devices mentioned.

Family Planning Association (FPA), St Andrew's House, 27–35 Mortimer Street, London W1N 7RJ (01 636 7866)

Brook Advisory Centres, 233 Tottenham Court Road, London W1 9AE (01 580 2991, appointments, 01 323 1522 information)

Depression

Everyone feels low occasionally, sometimes because of a specific event but often for no very obvious reason. It is difficult to distinguish between true depression and a temporary loss of emotional equilibrium. If you realize that your unhappiness with life in general has started to outweigh your enjoyment then you should certainly think about seeking expert help.

TREATMENT AVAILABLE
Go and talk things over with your GP first. S/he will be able to work out with you the extent of your depressive state and the

best way of dealing with it, and may prescribe a short course of antidepressant drugs, or refer you to a local hospital. Don't be frightened by this. Depressive illnesses are far more responsive to treatment than is generally known so there is absolutely no need to suffer needlessly.

SELF-HELP
If you feel you would rather try and tackle the problem singlehanded or with the backup of a self-help organization you may find the following addresses helpful.

Depressives Anonymous, 36, Chestnut Avenue, Beverley, North Humberside HU17 9QU A network of ten local groups which organizes fortnightly open meetings all over the UK and produces a quarterly newsletter.

Depressives Associated, PO Box 5, Castle Town, Portland DT5 1BQ A network of self-help mutual support groups in England with contacts in Ireland and Scotland. Also produces newsletters.

The Women's Therapy Centre, 6 Manor Gardens, London N7 6LA (01 263 6200) Also runs a workshop for women which explores ways of coping with feelings of depression.

Divorce

Divorce is a traumatic experience for anyone but permanent scars on you or your children can be prevented by getting yourself equipped with the best legal, practical and emotional support you can. All the following organizations offer information and counselling at any stage of the process of divorce and are particularly helpful in assisting parents to reach their own decisions in the best interests of their children.

The Family Courts Service, 2nd floor, 217a Balham High Road, London SW17 7BP (01-672 2682/8812)

Divorce Conciliation Advisory Services, 38 Ebury Street, London SW1W 0LU (01 730 2422) Free for those on social security or pensions with no source of income.

National Council for the Divorced and Separated, 13 High Street, Little Shelford, Cambridge CB2 5ES (01 300 4669 day, or 01 254 2080 evening) Promotes social activities through a nationwide network. Also runs holiday schemes. Counselling centres in several regions incorporating legal, financial, property and social services advice, postal advisory service.

Mothers Apart From Their Children (MATCH), BM Problems Ltd, London WC1N 1XX (0895 672510) Self-help group for mothers who have given up their children voluntarily and those who have lost custody. Provides support and practical advice. Also publishes newsletters and leaflets, available for a small fee.

National Family Conciliation Council, Mrs Jenny Bassett, 34 Milton Road, Swindon, Wilts SN1 5JA (0793 618486 information) A registered charity made up of a number of affiliated organizations offering a conciliation service to resolve disputes resulting from divorce, with particular reference to the care and emotional welfare of the children.

Families Need Fathers, 37, Garden Road London SE15 3UB (01 639 5362); Publications address: Dept CP, 39 Clonmore Avenue, Orpington, Kent BR6 9LE A nationwide society aiming to establish post-divorce close contact with children for both parents.

Family Service Units, 207, Old Marylebone Road, London NW1 5QP (01 402 5175) Offers support and counselling to families currently undergoing stress of any kind. National network.

Eating disorders

See Anorexia and Bulimia.

The elderly

Over 1.5 million people in Britain, of whom the majority are women, are today leading low-quality, high-stress lives as a result of looking after an elderly relative at home. It's not easy coping even with your own parents, particularly if there is a health problem, and you certainly need both the practical and emotional support the following organizations can give you.

The Association of Carers, Medway Homes, Balfour Road, Rochester, Kent NE4 6QU (0634 813981) Runs a network of self-help and support groups.

Age Concern, Bernard Sunley House, Pitcairn Road, Mitcham, Surrey CR4 3LL (01 640 5431) Offers a number of services, including trained volunteers who can provide short periods of relief, and day-care facilities.

Help The Aged, 16/18 St James Walk, London EC1R 0BE (01 253 0253) Basically a fund-raising and organizing society providing information and advice concerning good neighbour schemes, housing, day centres, work centres and mobile chiropody units. Also publishes newspapers.

Family planning

See Contraception

Genetic counselling

If you are the parent of a handicapped child, have reason to think that there may be some genetic abnormality in your family, or have suffered a stillbirth or several miscarriages, you and your partner may well be advised to undergo some form of genetic counselling.

TREATMENT AVAILABLE
Ask your GP to arrange this for you. An appointment will be

made at your local hospital for you and your partner as both your medical and family histories will require investigation. Medical tests will then be carried out in order to ensure that there are no genetic abnormalities on either side. The majority of couples are given the all-clear and there is usually no need for any follow-up.

If any serious abnormality should be discovered there are various self-help groups which have been set up for the sufferers of the more serious hereditary diseases and their families.

Brent Sickle Cell Centre, Willesden Hospital, Harlesden Road, London NW10 3RY (01 459 1292, Ext 4235)

Combat – Association to Combat Huntington's Chorea, 34a Station Road, Hinckley, Leicester, LE10 1AP (0455 615558)

Family Counselling Service, Shirley Dalby, ACHC Family Counselling Service, 108 Battersea High Street, London SW11 3HP (01 223 7000) Visits can be made to families or you can visit their London office. Welfare service and holiday homes available as well as genetic counselling service. Information sheets and short-term holiday bookings also available on request.

United Kingdom Thalassaemia Society, 107 Nightingale Lane, London N8 7QY (01 348 0437) Education, information and counselling (general and genetic) for all those who are concerned that they or members of their families may be suffering from or be genetic carriers of thalassaemia. Publicity available in English, Greek, Turkish and the main Asian languages.

Infertility

Doubts about your ability to reproduce can pose a major threat to happiness and emotional stability. Infertility affects approximately 15 per cent of the population and can stem from a variety of curable and incurable conditions in both male and female. The problem may be with one partner within a couple or it may be the result of a combination of factors from both sides.

Investigation into the cause of infertility will involve a series of tests on both partners to try to trace the point at which the process of conception is being obstructed. It is very important that you also receive sympathetic and supportive counselling throughout this process in order to be able to deal with any difficult feelings (such as guilt, anger or resentment) that may arise as a result of the tests. You may also need help in coming to terms with the various options open to you as a couple if your particular problem turns out to be untreatable.

TREATMENT AVAILABLE

Your doctor will probably suggest that you try for at least six months before advising any investigation. He can then refer you either to your local NHS hospital (waiting lists vary depending on where you live) or privately. The major causes of infertility in a woman are:

1. The ovary may not be producing a mature egg.
2. The egg may not be being drawn into the Fallopian tube.
3. Involuntary muscular spasm of the vaginal muscles may be preventing penetration.
4. The tubes may be blocked preventing the passage of both eggs and sperm.
5. The shape of the womb may be affecting the woman's ability to retain the foetus.
6. Absence of the cervical mucus, or a mucus which is hostile to sperm may be preventing fertilization.
7. Scar tissue may be sticking down the tubes and ovaries (adhesions) or groups of cells similar to those lining the uterus may be present (endometriosis).

In a man the main causes of infertility are:

1. The testes failing to produce enough normal, healthy sperm.
2. Tight foreskin making penetration painful.
3. Failure to achieve erection.
4. Premature ejaculation and abnormalities of the penis.

5. Abnormality of the urethra causing semen to pass into the bladder.
6. The vasa may either be blocked or nonexistent.

Don't despair if neither hormonal treatment nor surgery is found to be the answer to your particular problem. *In vitro* fertilization (the test-tube baby technique) has proved itself a successful alternative for some women, although it remains a highly complicated and delicate operation in which the results certainly cannot be guaranteed. What happens is that a number of mature eggs are removed from the woman's ovary and fertilized by the man's sperm in the laboratory. Once it has been established that the fertilized egg is developing normally it is replaced in the womb to continue its growth in the ordinary way. It sounds simple but things can go wrong with the implantation for reasons that are as yet not fully understood. Private clinics claim a slightly higher success rate than the NHS (at best it is only 15 per cent) but treatment can be expensive at approximately £1000 for each attempt.

The most recent innovation in the test-tube technique is known as GIFT (Gamete Intra-Fallopian Transfer). This has the advantage of the fertilization actually taking place within the woman's body and has had a success rate of 25–35 per cent in selected cases. This procedure differs from IVF in that the egg and sperm are replaced in the Fallopian tube rather than the uterus (it is obviously essential that the woman should have at least one fully functioning Fallopian tube for this to work). As fertilization has taken place in the body rather than outside it, and the egg has travelled to the womb in the normal way the GIFT stands a better chance of successful implantation. Top specialists believe GIFT to be of limited value in the long-term outlook for the treatment of women's infertility, and are searching to discover why the chemical factors in the Fallopian tube should improve the fertilized egg's chance of survival, so that they can facilitate the reproduction of these conditions in the laboratory.

As GIFT requires the same degree of surgery, drugs and specialized medical supervision, it is unfortunately just as expensive as IVF treatment.

If your particular problem will not react to treatment you may like to consider adoption as an alternative. Don't rush into anything – remember that wanting a child of your own is not the same as electing to bring up someone else's. Everyone's feelings need to come under consideration, not least those of your partner and, most importantly, the child itself.

If it is your partner who is infertile you could also consider the possibility of AID (Artificial Insemination by Donor). This has received much adverse publicity as a result of the moral and legal implications highlighted in recent controversial surrogate motherhood cases. In fact AID has been practised in this country for over forty years and, for some people, provides a wonderful chance of overcoming an infertility problem that might ultimately destroy an otherwise satisfying and fulfilling partnership.

The service is also available to women without a partner. Treatment consists of the insertion of semen in the mucus at the neck of the womb by a doctor or nurse. Inseminations are charted to coincide with the woman's most likely period of ovulation. The procedure is safe, simple and painless. Contact any of the following addresses for further information.

The British Pregnancy Advisory Service (Head Office), Austry Manor, Wootton Wawen, Solihull, West Midlands B95 6BX (056 42 3225)

Pregnancy Advisory Service, 11–13 Charlotte Street, London W1P 1HD (01 637 8962)

British Agencies for Adoption and Fostering (BAAF), 11 Southwark Street, London SE1 1RQ (01 407 8800) Advisory service for member agencies, students and the public. Also publishes booklets on adoption.

The Post Adoption Centre, Gregory House, 48 Mecklenburgh Square, London WC1N 2NU (01 833 3214.) Set up to help families in the process of adoption either before or after the event.

Isolation

Any problem, whether emotional or practical, seems worse when there is no one you can talk it over with. The more entrenched in loneliness you become, the more difficult it is to break down those imaginary boundaries and make human contact again. The sooner you act positively the better for your emotional health and happiness.

SELF-HELP GROUPS
National Federation of Solo Clubs, Room 8, Ruskin Chambers, 191, Corporation Street, Birmingham B4 6RY (021 236 2879) Organizes clubs for divorced, separated, widowed and single people between the ages of twenty-five and sixty-five.

Gay Switchboard, BM Switchboard, London WC1 3XX (01 837 7324) 24-hour information and help service for lesbians and gay men. Will also refer recently bereaved to the Gay Bereavement Project.

Contact, 15 Henrietta Street, London WC2E 8QH (01 240 0630 9.30a.m. - 5.30p.m. Mon – Fri and 24-hour answering service) Contact groups for the isolated elderly throughout the UK. Also organizes monthly outings.

Wider Horizons, 'Westbrook', Back Lane, Malvern, Hereford and Worcester WR14 2HJ (06845 64462) Encourages the broadening of interests among lonely, housebound or elderly people by promoting opportunities for new interests, friendships and exchange of information between members. Also provides information on holidays, hobbies, welfare and special aids.

Marriage guidance

Whatever the nature of your particular problem as a couple there is no need to give up on a potentially good relationship without a struggle. There are sympathetic and caring experienced

148

counsellors out there who can sometimes help to clear tangled communication lines. Never patronizing, a good marriage counsellor or therapist will simply reflect the intimate feelings that you may both have found difficult either to identify or articulate. Once the main cause of marital conflict has been recognized, a peace treaty becomes at least a possibility.

National Marriage Guidance Council, Herbert Gray College, Little Church Street, Rugby, Warwickshire CV21 3AP (0778 73214) Central coordinating body for network of local Marriage Guidance Councils offering counselling for anyone seeking help with a relationship whether married or single and of whatever sexual persuasion. Also refers couples with psychosexual problems to specially trained counsellors. Local office in telephone directory.

Brook Advisory Centre (Head Office), 233 Tottenham Court Road, London W1 9AE (01 580 2991 appointments, 01 323 1552 information) Offers confidential advice and counselling as well as contraceptive information to the under-twenty-five age group.

Tavistock Institute of Medical Psychology, Tavistock Centre, Belsize lane, London NW3 5BA (01 435 7111) Offers marriage guidance on the NHS through its Marital Unit or fee-paying therapy through the Institute of Marital Studies. Both can be contacted through the above telephone number.

Catholic Marriage Council, 23, Ravenshurst Avenue, London NW4 4EL (01 203 6311)

Menopause

You don't have to suffer in silence. Whether your problem is physical, emotional or a confusing mixture of the two there is help available. If your doctor is sympathetic s/he may refer you to one of the many hospital clinics now dealing specifically in menopausal problems. Alternatively, get in contact with:

149

MidLife Centre, 318 Summer Lane, Birmingham, B19 3RL
(021359 3563) Campaigns for a better understanding of midlife
anxieties. It also offers personal advice on potential crises such as
career change, mental approach to the menopause, preretirement, and how to cope with a change of lifestyle. Also publishes
regular newspaper.

Women's Therapy Centre, 6 Manor Gardens, London N7 6LA
(01 263 6200) Also runs a workshop where women can share
both their experiences and information about the menopause as
well as learning ways of coping with growing older.

Menstruation

Approximately once a month the lining of the womb builds up a
protective layer of blood in preparation for receiving the ripening
egg if it is fertilized. If the fusion of the egg and sperm does not
take place, this lining then proceeds to break up and dissolves in
the blood that is passed out through the vagina.

Many women have longer or shorter gaps than twenty-eight
days and unless there is a possibility of pregnancy, or a regular
cycle suddenly becomes disrupted, there is no need to worry
about the timing of menstruation.

Various factors can cause such disruption. Being substantially
under or overweight, stress and depression can all suppress
ovulation (egg production), so if periods are absent for more than
six months, it's certainly worth seeing a doctor. Often the
reassurance that nothing is wrong is enough to bring back a
regular pattern. Coming off the Pill or breastfeeding a baby,
particularly for any length of time, can also temporarily interrupt
the menstrual cycle.

Usually any unpleasant symptoms or pain start to decrease at
the onset of the actual blood flow. A sensible diet (high fibre, low
salt and sugar and plenty of fresh fruit) can also relieve the
common problem of constipation, as can some form of active
sport like cycling or swimming.

Muscular tension as a result of anxiety intensifies period pains, so relaxation is vital. Regular breathing exercises are useful for controlling this.

National Association for Pre-Menstrual Syndrome. 25 Market Street, Guildford, Surrey GU1 4LB (0483 572715) Helpline: (0483 572806, Mon – Fri) Self-help groups for sufferers from pre-menstrual syndrome and post-natal depression. Membership £5 p.a. Nationwide network of contacts plus useful information.

Miscarriage (See also Bereavement and Stillbirth)

The majority of miscarriages occur early in pregnancy, sometimes before pregnancy has been suspected, but as early pregnancy tests have now become increasingly sensitive, they still remain a severe emotional shock for many women. Older and first-time mothers are slightly more prone to suffer them but having one does not necessarily mean a greater risk of having a second one.

During the first twelve weeks of pregnancy the first sign of threatened miscarriage is a small amount of bleeding similar to the onset of a period. This may last several days and cease of its own accord in which case the pregnancy will probably continue quite normally. If there are pains or cramping it may be developing into a full-blown miscarriage (also known as a threatened abortion).

Doctors don't really know why it happens but in many cases there has been a hitch in the complicated process of implantation and early development, or possibly some chromosomal disorder, in which case your body is protecting you from giving birth to an abnormal child. For this reason medical opinion is divided as to how far to go in trying to prevent a potential miscarriage. Some women miscarry because of the presence of fibroids in the womb, or because the cervix (neck of the womb) has been stretched too much by an earlier pregnancy. Hormonal imbalance is yet another possible cause.

Hormonal imblance can be easily rectified by taking blood samples and screening hormone levels throughout the monthly cycle. Your doctor can refer you for this at your local NHS hospital. Fibroids can be quite simply removed, whilst it is possible for an enlarged or weak cervix to be stitched up until a week or two before delivery.

If you have suffered recurrent miscarriages for no apparent cause, further investigations may need to be carried out on both you and your partner. You may also be referred for genetic counselling. Don't be alarmed by this. It is merely a sensible precaution and the procedure is completely painless. (See also Genetic counselling).

SELF-HELP

Doctors cannot seem to agree as to how influential the factor of stress may be on the threatened miscarriage but it would certainly seem wise to avoid it as far as is humanly possible.

Giving up smoking, drinking and any over-strenuous sport is also a good idea, although gentle exercise will improve the health of a hopeful mother-to-be. It is best to consult your doctor as to the degree of exercise suitable for your particular circumstances (including the frequency of sexual intercourse).

The Miscarriage Association, 11 Bank Street, Ossett, West Yorks (0924 85515) Offers advice and support for women suffering from or recovering after the experience of a miscarriage. Can refer to local groups and also publishes pamphlets and a regular newsletter.

National Association for the Childless, 318, Summer Lane, Birmingham B19 3RL (021 359 4887) Offers advice and inform-ation on infertility, artificial insemination, miscarriage, adoption and fostering as well as aiming to help couples to adapt them-selves, if necessary, to living as full a life as possible without children.

Psychosexual problems

The more intimate a problem the more difficult it can be to confront, particularly with the one other person most closely concerned. The wrong words can act as a tripwire in an 'explosive' sexual situation and can often make relations even worse. Most people still find the language of sex either humorous or highly embarrassing. Neither reaction is conducive to resolving sensitive issues satisfactorily. There is no need to suffer in silence. There is help at hand whether you are single, living with someone, or married, and whatever your age or sexual experience.

COMMON PROBLEMS
One of the most frightening aspects of a psychosexual problem is the fact that we imagine ourselves to be the only person in the world affected by it. Impotence, premature ejaculation, vaginismus (involuntary contraction of the muscles of the vagina), and the inability to reach orgasm are all far more common than we realize. They also give rise to a great number of emotional difficulties, anxiety, depression and unhappiness, if nothing is done to relieve them.

TREATMENT AVAILABLE
A confidential chat with your GP can be very reassuring if s/he is sensitive enough to be able to overcome any natural reticence or embarrassment on either side. Not all doctors have necessarily had any training or experience in dealing with patients' sexual difficulties so you may well find yourself being referred on to the Association of Sexual and Marital Therapists or to a Marriage Guidance Council sexual dysfunction clinic. Alternatively, if you don't feel happy about talking to your doctor you can approach either of these organizations directly without a letter of referral.

Don't be inhibited by their dramatic titles. All those who work in the field of sexual medicine are sympathetic and experienced in dealing with men and women in distress. Their first concern will be in creating an atmosphere in which you feel relaxed enough to reveal your worries comfortably. Once the possibility of any physical basis for your problem has been eliminated, treatment mainly involves learning to talk to each other frankly about sexual likes and dislikes, and discovering the importance of touching and stroking, not only as a precursor to full penetration but as a valuable form of lovemaking in its own right. Couples are often asked to hold back from full intercourse whilst practising these exercises in order to relieve the pressure on performance and to concentrate instead on both giving and receiving pleasure.

Human beings do not come off a production line – any advice or suggestions on improving your sex-life will be uniquely tailored to your particular problem. There are many causes for sexual difficulty. Finding a successful solution involves retaining a flexible approach. Contact any of the following for more information.

The Association of Sexual and Marital Therapists, PO Box 621 Sheffield 10 Has a nationwide list of reputable practitioners.

National Marriage Guidance Council, Herbert Gray College, Little Church Street, Rugby, Warwickshire CV21 3AP (0788 73241) Will refer to their sexual dysfunction clinics. Check in the phone directory under Marriage Guidance for the council nearest you.

Association to Aid the Sexual and Personal Relationships of the Disabled (SPOD), 286 Camden Road, London N7 OBJ (01 607 8851/2)

Postnatal depression

It's not permanent and you're not going mad. Giving birth is an emotional and physical trauma. Looking after yourself should be your number one priority if you are going to be able to take care of your child properly. Don't hesitate to ask for help – there are hundreds of women out there feeling exactly the same way. Hoping it will go away on its own is not a satisfactory answer. Act positively to dispel it and stop it from interfering in your enjoyment of this time.

Talk to your GP or contact one of the following organizations.

The Association for Postnatal Illness, 7 Gowar Avenue, London SW6 6RH (01 731 4867) This is a national network of phone and postal volunteers who have all experienced and recovered from postnatal depression. Free leaflets describing some of the more common symptons of this distressing condition.

Meet-a-Mum Association (MAMA), c/o Kate Goodyer, 3 Woodside Avenue, South Norwood, London SE25 5DW (01 654 3137) This is a self-help organization for new mothers, or those with young children, who may be suffering from fatigue, depression or isolation. Runs a nationwide advice network organizing social gatherings and local support groups.

The National Childbirth Trust, 9 Queensborough Terrace, London W2 3TB (01 221 3833) Promotes happy and anxiety-free experience of childbirth plus advice on how to prepare for parenthood. Countrywide contact groups who run antenatal classes, postnatal support groups, and breastfeeding counsellors. Also offers counselling for those distressed by miscarriages or Caesarian births, and the special problems of working mothers. Publishes a wide-ranging list of inexpensive leaflets on relevant topics.

Pregnancy (see also Postnatal depression)

Having a baby is not always so blissful and emotionally trouble-free an experience as the books and brochures suggest. Doctors now recommend that you begin preparing yourself for childbirth at least three months before conception by taking such sensible health precautions as cutting down on drinking, eliminating smoking and making sure you are getting an adequate diet.

The more informed you are about the various delivery options open to you, the more chance you will have of enjoying a happy and successful labour, so do find out as much as you can beforehand. Make sure you have practical and emotional backup at hand in the form of friends, family or one of the various support groups listed below.

The Active Birth Centre, 18 Laurier Road, London NW5 1SD (01 267 3006) Promotes the provision of a happy mean between 'high-tech' and natural births. Also runs antenatal breathing and relaxation classes with the emphasis on personal responsibility. Information service is free. Mail order book service also available.

Association for Improvement in the Maternity Services (AIMS), c/o Hon Secretary, 163 Liverpool Road, London N1 0RF (01 278 5628) Provides advice and information on all aspects of maternity services and childcare for prospective parents. Twelve branches spread throughout the country. Also produces information leaflets and a quarterly bulletin.

The Association of Radical Midwives (ARMS), c/o 8a The Drive, Wimbledon, London SW20 8TG (01 504 2010)

Caesarean Support Group, 7 Green Street, Willingham Cambridge CB4 5JA (0954 60630) Organizes phone and postal advice, counselling and support, both before and after operation. Network of contact groups nationwide. Also publishes leaflets on the experience of Caesarean birth and breastfeeding.

La Leche League of Great Britain, Box 3424, London WC1 6XX (01 883 7801) Offers advice and sympathetic support to would-be breastfeeders from women who have successfully breastfed in the past. Also organizes meetings and has a telephone link service.

Maternity Alliance, 59–61, Camden High Street, London NW1 7JL (01 388 6337) Offers a wide range of services including advice on maternity benefits and preconceptual care. Also publishes leaflets.

Retirement

This can be a fulfilling time of reassessment and renewal if you allow it to be. Retirement is as potentially rewarding and exciting as the rest of life, depending on how you interpret your talents or the opportunities available to you.

There are also bound to be times when you feel alone and sad either through the loss or ill health of old friends or a natural sadness at the thought of approaching old age. There's no need to feel useless and discarded. Preretirement planning is becoming increasingly common and is a very good way of avoiding the depression and anxiety that is so easy to fall prey to after an active middle age.

Employment Fellowship, 'Willowthorpe', High Street, Stanstead Abbotts, nr Ware, Herts SG12 8AS (0920 870158) This organization runs a nationwide network of retirement workshops and centres as well as employment bureaux to assist people both in finding employment and making the most of their leisure time. It also helps in starting up neighbourhood community care schemes to help the housebound.

The Pre-Retirement Association of Great Britain and Northern Ireland, 19, Undine Street, London SW17 8PP (01 767 3225) Offers advice and information on retirement planning (including the best way of preparing yourself emotionally for it), finance, housing, health and leisure activities. Information, advice service and book list is free to members. Also runs preretirement courses.

REACH (Retired Executives Action Clearing House), 89 Southwark Street, London SE1 OHD (01 928 0452) Free (expenses only) employment service which puts retired executives in touch with charitable organizations needing help.

Success After Sixty, 40–41 Old Bond Street, London W1X 3AF (01 629 0672) or 33 George Street, Croydon, Surrey CRO 1LB (01 680 0858) Employment agency catering mainly for office staff which assists those of fifty plus in finding jobs as well as offering advice on ways in which earning affects pensions. Fees are charged to employers only.

Sexually transmitted diseases (see also AIDS)

If you think you may have contracted an infection, don't hesitate to go straight to your doctor or clinic. Apart from AIDS, all sexually transmitted diseases are now curable but it is vital to get treatment quickly before any irreparable damage may be done to your reproductive organs. Many a case of infertility could have been avoided by prompt attention to such symptoms as heavy vaginal discharge or irritation.

GONORRHOEA
Women often show no symptoms at all. In men the disease usually shows up as a yellow discharge from the penis within three to ten days of infection.

SYPHILIS
The first sign is a painless sore on the vulva in women or the penis in men. Symptoms start to appear between nine and ninety days of infection. The disease is detected by a clinic blood test.

HERPES
Virus produces coldsore-like blisters in the genital area about a week after infection. These may be accompanied by a feeling of feverishness, swollen glands, tenderness or itching, and pain on passing urine.

NON-SPECIFIC URETHRITIS (NSU)
This causes inflammation of the urethra in both men and women and has an incubation period of seven to fourteen days. The symptoms are pain when passing urine and discharge from bladder opening in women or the penis in men.

TRICHOMONIASIS
Very common in women. Symptoms show up seven to twenty-eight

days after infection. There may be no obvious symptoms at all or possibly an unpleasant-smelling yellow discharge, pain during sex, irritation and redness of the vulva (or penis); and a possible outbreak of cystitis.

CYSTITIS
An inflammation of the lining of the bladder and urethra. Symptoms are increased frequency of urination accompanied by a burning sensation, possible blood or pus in the urine and low back pain.

THRUSH
An inflammation of the vulva, vagina or anus mainly affecting women. It is caused by a yeast or fungus known as Candida. Symptoms are a thick white discharge, irritation or soreness and possibly painful intercourse.

PELVIC INFLAMMATORY DISEASE/(PID)
Any infection which has managed to spread beyond the genital area to the reproductive organs. It can lead to scarring and blocking of the Fallopian tubes so prompt attention is essential. Symptoms are pain in the abdomen or lower back, vaginal discharge, nausea, heavy or irregular periods and fever or fatigue.

TREATMENT AVAILABLE
Go to your GP or local STD clinic (often called genito-urinary clinic). The nearest address and telephone number is in the phonebook. All personal information given is strictly confidential and staff are sympathetic and kind. Most of the infections mentioned are quite simply treated with a short course of antibiotics after which you will be required to return for a final all-clear examination.

Single parents

Every parent has to cope with a certain amount of physical and emotional strain, but being a single parent often seems to more than double the burden. You simultaneously become both carer and sole provider, and are expected by your children to be both omnipotent and on tap 24 hours a day. Under these circumstances, it's often extremely difficult to get any time or space to yourself. Yet building an independent existence is vital both to the successful survival of the single-parent family and to everyone's sanity. Financial and emotional security should be your first priorities. Any of the following one-parent organizations can help with advice and information on welfare rights and benefits available, as well as providing essential social contacts and details of holiday schemes for the rest and relaxation you will need.

Gingerbread, 35, Wellington Street, London WC2E 7BN (01 240 0953) Runs over 350 self-help groups for one-parent families throughout the UK. Also provides social contacts for adults and children as well as practical advice and information.

Single Parent Links and Special Holidays (SPLASH) 19, North Street, Plymouth PL4 9AH (0752 674067) Gives details on holiday schemes available to single-parent families.

The National Council for One-Parent Families, 255 Kentish Town Road, London NW5 2LX (01 267 1361) Confidential advice and information to single parents and pregnant women on everything you may need to know concerning welfare rights, housing, childcare facilites and help with emotional problems.

Step-parents

Expectations of instant love from your stepfamily are doomed to disappointment. If it takes time to build up emotional bonds in a natural family, you cannot expect strangers to hit it off straightaway. Talking to others who have been through the experience may help you to steer clear of the more dangerous emotional landmines such as feelings of inadequacy or guilt, jealousy of the previous partner and/or their children as well as loss of privacy and possible resulting sexual tension.

Stepfamily (The National Stepfamily Association), 162 Tennison Road, Cambridge CB1 2DP (0223 460312/460313 counselling) This organization provides a network of self-help discussion groups throughout the UK. Also links up stepfamilies to help each other work out the initial problems that a new partnership may have. An emergency and telephone counselling service is available to members as well as a regular newsletter and information booklets.

Grandmothers' Ginger Group, c/o Mrs Shirley Hefferman, 15 Calder Close, Plymouth, Devon A group of supportive grandparents who wish to keep in close contact with their grandchildren after the remarriage of their children. Active in trying to change the law in order to grant statutory access to grandparents all over the UK.

National Marriage Guidance Council, Little Church Street, Rugby CV21 3AP (0788 73241) In addition to its excellent services for couples in distress the NMGC are always willing to discuss family problems. Also publish a quarterly bulletin.

Stillbirth (see also Miscarriage and Bereavement)

Advances in medical science have meant that this is now relatively rare but statistics don't help to relieve the distress if it should happen to you.

Stillbirth is a very traumatic experience. Recognizing that fact and allowing yourself time to grieve for the lost child is vital to emotional recovery.

'Stillbirth' is a blanket term both for those babies who have already died in the womb and for those who die at birth. The most common causes for foetal death are:

1. 'Anoxia' or lack of oxygen, usually due to the umbilical cord becoming compressed or caught around the baby's neck.
2. The placenta, which provides the baby with its nourishment, may have started to deteriorate. This starts to become a danger

once the baby is more than two weeks overdue.

3. Pre-eclampsia toxaemia (high-blood pressure) can effect the flow of blood between mother and baby; the main symptoms of this potentially very dangerous condition are:

(i) high blood pressure

(ii) protein in the urine

(iii) oedema (fluid retention)

If left untreated this can result in miscarriage, permanent damage to the mother's kidneys, and in extreme cases, the death of both mother and baby.

4. Respiratory distress, more common amongst premature babies, as a result of the shock of birth.

5. Congenital abnormality.

TREATMENT AVAILABLE

Regular attendance at antenatal clinics will ensure that any medical problems are picked up early enough to be safely corrected as well as providing the emotional backup of other mothers-to-be.

Amniocentesis (whereby a sample of the amniotic fluid surrounding the foetus is drawn out and tested for abnormalities such as Down's syndrome) has now become very advanced. This screening process can offer the mother of a potentially handicapped child the option of terminating the pregnancy.

New obstetric technology now enables doctors to monitor labour very closely so that intervention is immediate if the foetus starts showing the slightest signs of distress. This has helped enormously in cutting down the number of foetal deaths.

SELF-HELP

As in the prevention of any miscarriage, looking after yourself by making sure you have a good diet and the right mix of rest and exercise is the best way of protecting your child.

The Stillbirth and Neo-Natal Death Association, Argyle House, 29–31 Euston Road, London NW1 2SD (01 833 2851) Provides information and support-group contacts for bereaved parents.

The Compassionate Friends, 6 Denmark Street, Bristol, BS1 5DQ (0272 292778) Organizes home visits and meetings for bereaved parents. A leaflet is also available.

The Pre-Eclamptic Toxaemia Society, Mrs. Sharon Copping, Eaton Lodge, 8 Southend Road, Hockley, Essex (0702 205088) Support, information and self-help group. Annual membership £3.00.

Tranquillizer dependency

Taking tranquillizers can seem a great relief when you first start but if you are finding it more and more difficult to do without them, or if you have tried and failed due to your unpleasant withdrawal symptoms (often distressingly similar to those which first led you to take them) it's time for action.

You may be feeling that you just cannot cope without them. If so, it's well worth realizing, through listening to other people's experiences, that tranquillizer addiction can be conquered. It's tough initially but eventually the day will dawn when you can feel 'normal' and happy without any artificial aids.

TREATMENT AVAILABLE
If you have a good relationship with your GP, try talking to him about your problem first. Personal responsibility is now the current watchword for women's health but coming off tranquillizers safely requires medical supervision. Here your doctor can help by prescribing similar pills of lower dosage.

SELF-HELP
Community Drug Project, 30 Manor Place, London SE17 3BB (01 703 0559) Offers advice, information and counselling to addicts both of illegal and prescribed legal drugs. Provides support and practical help to families and will refer on to local self-help groups.

Tranquillizer Recovery and New Existence (TRANX), 17 Peel

Road, Harrow, Middlesex, HA3 7QX (01 427 2065) Publishes handbook on starting self-help groups as well as offering advice and counselling to addicts. Holds weekly meetings.

Drugs, Alcohol, Women, Nationally, (DAWN), Omnibus Workspace, 39–41, North Road, London N7 GDP (01 700 4653) London only. Keeps list of available facilities for women. Organizes workshops on addiction and dependency as well as providing leaflets. Open meeting held every six weeks.

Women's health (general)

London Women's Aid Federation of England, PO Box 391, Bristol BX99 7SW (0272 420611) and 52–54 Featherstone Street, London EC3 (01-251 6537/8 01-253 2033 24-hour answering service) Network of groups which provide temporary accommodation in refuges for women and children who suffer physical, mental and/or sexual abuse. Also offers advice and support.

Women's Alcohol Centre, 254 St Paul's Road, London N1 2LJ (01 226 4581) Confidential service for women with drink problems. Offers individual and group counselling, crèche facilities and practical advice. Residential support sometimes possible.

Women's Health Concern (WHC), Ground Floor Flat, 17 Earls Terrace, London W8 6LP (01 602 6669) Registered charity offering personalized medical advice as well as professional counselling at all levels. Also publishes a wide range of pamphlets concerning women's health and related social issues.

Women's National Cancer Control Campaign, 1 South Audley Street, London W1 Y5 DQ (01 499 7532) Offers help and advice on prevention and early detection of breast and cervical cancer. Can also refer to Well Woman clinics and other centres for tests. Fleet of five mobile units for screening which are available both to companies and the general public.

Women's Therapy Centre, 6 Manor Gardens, London N7 6LA (01 263 6200) Offers counselling and psychotherapy for women and their families by women counsellors/therapists. Wide range of workshops on women's issues.

Hysterectomy Support Group, c/o Ann Webb, 11 Henryson Road, Brockley, London SE4 1HL (01 690 5987) A network of self-help support groups run by women who have had hysterectomies themselves. Will refer to contact addresses. Also publishes newsletters.

Breast Care and Mastectomy Association, 26 Harrison Street, London WC1 8JG (01 837 0908) Nonmedical organization providing information concerning both pre- and post-mastectomy care. Also runs support system of women who have had mastectomies themselves. Publishes advice leaflets on bras, prostheses and swimwear.

Women's Nutritional Advisory Service, PO Box 268, Hove, East Sussex BN3 1RW Postal service offering advice and information packs on the prevention of premenstrual, postnatal and menopausal emotional problems through adequate nutrition. Charges fee but follows up patients after three months.

Reading List

Understanding Women Susie Orbach and Luise Eichenbaum, Penguin 1985

What Do Women Want? Susie Orbach and Luise Eichenbaum, Fontana 1984

The Female Eunuch Germaine Greer, Paladin 1971

Passages Gail Sheehy, Bantam 1982

Babyshock John Cobb, Hutchinson 1980

The Millstone Margaret Drabble, Weidenfeld and Nicholson 1965

The Women's Room Marilyn French, Sphere 1968

Social Trends HMSO 1987

Index

Index compiled by Peva Keane